THE HAMMARSKJÖLD FORUMS

Case Studies

on

The Role of Law

in the

Settlement of International Disputes

When Battle Rages, How Can Law Protect?

Working Paper and Proceedings of

The Fourteenth Hammarskjöld Forum

Howard S. Levie

Author of the Working Paper

John Carey

Editor

Published for
The Association of the Bar of the City of New York

by
Oceana Publications, Inc.
Dobbs Ferry, New York

1971

Library of Congress Catalog Card Number: 78-123998

International Standard Book Number 0-379-11814-9

MANUFACTURED IN THE UNITED STATES OF AMERICA

DEDICATED TO

JAMES N. ROSENBERG

1874 – 1970

THE FOURTEENTH HAMMARSKJÖLD FORUM

March 16, 1970

Participants

John Carey, presiding
*Chairman, Special Committee on the Lawyer's Role
in the Search for Peace, The Association of
the Bar of the City of New York*

Marc Schreiber
Director, Human Rights Division, United Nations

Howard S. Levie
*Professor, St. Louis University Law School
Colonel, U.S. Army (ret.)*

Richard R. Baxter
*Professor, Harvard Law School,
Colonel, U.S. Army (ret. res.)*

Richard D. McCarthy
*Member of Congress, Buffalo, New York.
Author of "The Ultimate Folly: War by Pestilence,
Asphyxiation and Defoliation"*

Table of Contents

SELECTED BIBLIOGRAPHY ON THE LAWS OF WAR
AS THEY AFFECT THE INDIVIDUAL

Editor's Foreword

The second anniversary of the My Lai massacre was marked by a Hammarskjöld Forum at The Association of the Bar of the City of New York, the fourteenth in the series. It seemed fitting on that occasion to address the problem of protection of the individual in times of armed conflict.

An outstanding working paper, included in this volume, was produced by one of the Forum participants, Professor Howard S. Levie. Since the United Nations was studying the same problem under the title of "Respect for Human Rights in Armed Conflict," the head of the U.N. Human Rights Division, Mr. Marc Schreiber, was asked to describe the work of his office. The Secretariat study theretofore published in Document A/7720 (1969) was later supplemented in Document A/8052 (1970). The General Assembly adopted no less than five resolutions on the subject in 1970. Further U.N. action is anticipated following study in 1971 by the International Committee of the Red Cross.

The other two Forum participants were Harvard Law Professor Richard R. Baxter, now Editor-in-Chief of the *American Journal of International Law,* and Congressman Richard D. McCarthy, author of a book on chemical and biological warfare. Comments from a Forum guest, New Zealand Professor R.Q. Quentin-Baxter, are also included here. The remainder of the book consists of a most useful bibliography prepared by Mr. Anthony Grech, the Librarian of The Association of the Bar of the City of New York.

The Association mourns the recent loss of one of its most distinguished members, Mr. James N. Rosenberg, who inspired and sustained the series of Hammarskjöld Forums. This volume is dedicated to him in grateful memory of his gentle but intense dedication to justice under law.

John Carey

SOME MAJOR INADEQUACIES IN THE EXISTING LAW RELATING TO THE PROTECTION OF INDIVIDUALS DURING ARMED CONFLICT

Howard S. Levie
Professor of Law, Saint Louis University School of Law

In a book published in 1954 the author said: "By 1907 the proportion of the laws of war embodied in general convention(s) far exceeded, and still exceeds to this day, that of the law of peace."[1] What he failed to mention was that, apart from the 1925 Geneva Protocol concerning gas and bacteriological warfare,[2] the conventional law of war relating to the conduct of hostilities dated (and still dates) from 1907;[3] and that there was not (and is not) a single piece of international legislation dealing specifically with what might well be considered a fairly important aspect of modern warfare—war in and from the air![4]

Shortly after the end of World War I an anonymous article appeared in the prestigious *British Yearbook of International Law* the thesis of which was that, the League of Nations having been established, it would be a "disastrous mistake" for the governments of member nations to use this new machinery to codify (or expand?) the law of war; and that the past failure of international law to provide viable solutions to the problems of peace was, at least in part, due to the preoccupation of writers and statesmen with the law of war and their consequent neglect of the law of peace.[5] Two arguments were advanced: first, that inasmuch as war had been abolished, there was no longer anything for the law of war to regulate;[6] and second, that in any event there was no point in wasting time and energy on rules of war because such rules would only be broken.[7] These arguments did not go unchallenged;[8] but that they prevailed with the majority of statesmen and international lawyers of the day is evident from the fact that the Third Hague Peace Conference, which had not been convened because of the advent of World War I, was never called into session and, despite the tremendous technological advances demonstrated during that war, the Regulations attached to the Fourth Hague Convention of 1907[9] continued to be the latest expression of States with respect to the conduct of hostilities.[10] Thus it was these Regulations, drafted in 1907, prior to the advent of such weapons as the tank and the airplane, weapons which had completely revolutionized warfare, which constituted the basic rules governing hostilities during World War II.

It could easily be assumed that the events of World War II would have caused a less antagonistic attitude towards efforts to modernize the law of war.[11] However, such was not the case. In a statement which could have been written by our anonymous post-World War I author and his adherents, the International Law Commission made the following decision at its 1949 organizational meeting:

> "18. The Commission considered whether the laws of war should be selected as a topic for codification. *It was suggested that, war having been outlawed, the regulation of its conduct had ceased to be relevant.* On the other hand, the opinion was expressed that, although the term 'laws of war' ought to be discarded, a study of the rules governing the use of armed force—legitimate or illegitimate—might be useful. . . . The majority of the Commission declared itself opposed to the study of the problem at the present stage. *It was considered that if the Commission, at the very beginning of its work, were to undertake this study, public opinion might interpret its action as showing lack of confidence in the efficiency of the means at the disposal of the United Nations for maintaining peace."*[12] (Emphasis added.)

As a result of that decision, and despite strong arguments in support of the need to modernize the law of war advanced by many of the leading international lawyers,[13] the Commission has, more than twenty years later, never of its own volition considered any aspect of the law of war. At the present time, then, we are compelled to apply to wars being fought in the eighth decade of the 20th century rules governing the conduct of hostilities which were drafted in the first decade of that century.[14] Just imagine the chaos if we were using the traffic regulations of that earlier horse-and-buggy decade to regulate today's traffic! Imagine Broadway and Forty-second Street with no traffic lights, no traffic policemen, no stop signs, and a five-mile per hour speed limit! But such are the rules under which the world community of nations, by its ostrich-like attitude, has permitted and continues to permit wars to be fought.[15]

Like the anonymous writer after World War I and like the International Law Commission after World War II, the United Nations itself has long been extremely reluctant to exert any effort toward modernizing the law of war for fear that public opinion might interpret such action as lack of confidence in that organization's ability to maintain the peace.[16] But more recently there is evidence that the General Assembly is becoming increasingly realistic in its approach to this problem and that humanitarian considerations are, at long last, having an effect. The International Conference on Human Rights, meeting in Teheran in May 1968, adopted a resolution which requested the General Assembly to invite the Secretary-General to study

> "the need for additional humanitarian international conventions or for possible revision of existing Conventions to ensure the better protection of civilians, prisoners and combatants in all armed conflicts and the prohibition and limitation of the use of certain methods and means of warfare."[17]

This Resolution, in turn, resulted in the adoption by the General Assembly of Resolution 2444 (XXIII);[18] the preparation of the study *Respect for Human Rights in Armed Conflict* by the Secretary-General;[19] and the adoption by the General Assembly on December 16, 1969, of Resolution 2597 (XXIV), the pertinent operative portions of which read as follows:

1. *Requests* the Secretary-General to continue the study initiated by resolution 2444 (XXIII), giving special attention to the need for protection of the rights of civilians and combatants in conflicts which arise from the struggles of peoples under colonial and foreign rule for liberation and self-determination and to the better application of existing humanitarian international conventions and rules to such conflicts;

2. *Requests* the Secretary-General to consult and cooperate closely with the International Committee of the Red Cross in regard to the studies being undertaken by that body on this question;

    *   *   *   *   *   *   *   *   *   *

5. *Decides* to give the highest priority to this question at the twenty-fifth session of the General Assembly;

6. *Invites* the Secretary-General to present a further report on this subject to the General Assembly at its twenty-fifth session.[20]

As it will have been noted from the foregoing, there is another powerful force at work in this area—the International Committee of the Red Cross (ICRC).[21] Even during the arid period in the codification of the so-called "Hague" law of war[22] after World War I, the ICRC was successful in obtaining the convening of a diplomatic conference in Geneva in 1929 which not only redrafted the 1906 Geneva Convention,[23] but also drafted the first convention dealing exclusively with the subject of prisoners of war.[24] And in 1949, just shortly after the International Law Commission had reached its decision not to include the law of war on its agenda, another diplomatic conference was convened at Geneva at the instance of the ICRC and, based on many years of preparatory work by the ICRC, it drafted and adopted four humanitarian conventions, [25] including the first ever to deal exclusively with the protection of civilians.[26] Moreover, when Resolution 2444 (XXIII) was adopted by the General Assembly, its basis was a resolution which had been adopted at the XXth International Conference of the Red Cross at Vienna in 1965;[27] and at the XXIst International Conference of the Red Cross, held in Istanbul in September 1969, a number of relevant resolutions were adopted.[28] Assuredly, with the General Assembly and the ICRC acting together in a concerted effort to reach the identical goal, the prospect for the revision and modernization of the law of war may now be viewed with some minimum degree of optimism. Of course, there is a long international road to travel from proposals, to draft convention, to diplomatic conference, to signed convention, to ratification by a sufficiently large number of States, including the great powers, to make any such revision and modernization meaningful;[29] but the very willingness of the General Assembly to acknowledge that the problem exists is "a giant step forward for all mankind."

It is perhaps appropriate to mention at this point a suggestion which has been offered in order to make work in this area more palatable to those who have heretofore opposed it. This suggestion is that the term "armed conflict" be used as a substitute for the word "war" in the context of rules governing hostilities. It will be recalled that in the 1949 decision of the International Law Commission not to enter this field, those who opposed that decision suggested that the term "laws of war" be discarded.[30] The same suggestion is to be found in the ICRC's proposals and practice and is stated to be based upon the need "to take account of the deep aspiration of the peoples to see peace installed." [31] And the Report, A/7720, makes the same suggestion, but apparently for the perhaps more logical reason that "armed conflict" is a consider-

4

ably more all-inclusive term, and therefore less subject to dispute, than is "war."[32] Whatever the motivation, such a change appears to be essentially one of semantics, and there does not appear to be any substantive objection to it. Moreover, if it will reduce opposition to the project for the revision and modernization of the applicable law, it will have served a useful and beneficial purpose.[33] Accordingly, the balance of this paper will use the terms "armed conflict," "rules of armed conflict," and "law of armed conflict," and, except where speaking historically, will pointedly refrain from the use of such antiquated terms as "war," "rules of war," and "law of war"!

Assuming then that the time is approaching when affirmative steps will be taken to revise and modernize the law of armed conflict, the question is presented as to the specific areas in which such revision and modernization is needed. Any attempt to answer that question completely would probably necessitate a listing which would cover many pages and explanatory matter which would fill many tomes. This paper, as its title indicates, will be limited to several matters considered to be the major inadequacies relating to the protection of individuals during armed conflict which presently exist and require correction. They are:

1. The non-existence of and the need for a method for the automatic determination that a particular inter-State relationship requires the application of the law of armed conflict;[34]

2. The non-existence of and the need for a method which will ensure the presence in the territory of each party to an armed conflict of a Protecting Power or an international body with adequate authority to police compliance with the law of armed conflict;

3. The non-existence of and the need for a complete and total prohibition of the use in armed conflict of any and all categories of chemical and biological agents; and

4. The non-existence of and the need for a complete code governing the use of air power in armed conflict with emphasis on the outright prohibition of any type of bombing which has as its basic target the civilian population.

In the discussion of each of these inadequacies in the present law governing armed conflict, an effort will be made to show the nature of the particular inadequacy and why its exists and to

5

suggest possible remedies, with the caveat that the suggested remedies are not intended to exclude other, possibly more practical and practicable, solutions. In view of the very nature of the inadequacies discussed, there would appear to be little need to advance arguments as to why each is deemed of sufficient import to be considered a major inadequacy requiring a remedy.

1. *The non-existence of and the need for a method for the automatic determination that a particular inter-State relationship requires the application of the law of armed conflict.*

One of the major inadequacies of the present law of armed conflict is that there is in existence no method for the automatic issuance of an authoritative and effective determination that the relationship between two or more States has reached a point where that law should be applied.

Under Article 1 of the Third Hague Convention of 1907 hostilities were instituted by a "reasoned declaration of war or . . . an ultimatum with conditional declaration of war"; and under Article 2 of that Convention the belligerents had the duty to notify neutrals of the existence of a state of war.[35] Of course, were these provisions uniformly complied with by States, the problem under discussion would not exist. Unfortunately, more often than not they have been honored in the breach. In 1914, just seven years after they had become a part of international legislation, Germany attacked Belgium without a declaration of war and started a policy which has been followed all to frequently since then.[36] Moreover, a number of nations have denied the applicability of the law of war by the use of subterfuge or perversion of the facts. Thus, the Sino-Japanese conflict of the late 1930s was designated by Japan as a "police action" which, it was claimed, did not bring the law of war into effect; and in numerous other cases the applicability of the provisions of the 1907 Hague and of the 1929 Geneva Conventions was rejected on the mere basis of a denial of the existence of a state of war—despite clear and undeniable evidence to the contrary. Concerning this situation the ICRC later said:

". . . Since 1907 experience has shown that many armed conflicts, displaying all the characteristics of a war, may arise without being preceded by any of the formalities laid down in the Hague Convention. Furthermore, there have been many cases where Parties to a conflict have contested the legitimacy of the enemy Government and therefore

6

refused to recognize the existence of a state of war. In the same way, the temporary disappearance of sovereign States as a result of annexation or capitulation has been put forward as a pretext for not observing one or other of the humanitarian Conventions. It was necessary to find a remedy to this state of affairs . . ."[37]

As the problem had thus long been recognized, in preparing the so-called Stockholm draft conventions (the working papers for the 1949 Diplomatic Conference which drafted the four 1949 Geneva Conventions) the ICRC attempted to solve it by proposing the employment of a phrase making each Convention applicable "to all cases of declared war or any other armed conflict which may arise between two or more of the High Contracting Parties, even if the state of war is not recognized by one of them." This proposal was adopted by the Diplomatic Conference without change and without debate.[38]

A great feeling of accomplishment was engendered by the acceptance of this supposedly all-inclusive phrase by the Diplomatic Conference. The same ICRC study quoted above said of it:

"By its general character, this paragraph deprives belligerents, in advance, of the pretexts they might in theory put forward for evading their obligations. There is no need for a formal declaration of war, or for the recognition of a state of war, as preliminaries to the application of the Convention . . . The occurrence of *de facto* hostilities is sufficient . . . Any difference arising between two States and leading to the intervention of members of the armed forces is an armed conflict within the meaning of Article 2, even if one of the Parties denies the existence of a state of war. . . ."[39]

Unfortunately, it has not uniformly worked out this way in practice. Thus, for example, in Vietnam, where thousands of planes have been shot down, tens of thousands of human beings have been killed, and millions of rounds of ammunition have been expended, the position has been taken by North Vietnam that the humanitarian conventions governing armed conflict, to which she long ago acceded, do not apply.[40]

Thus, after World War II it was considered necessary to evolve a method which would make it impossible for States to engage in armed conflict and attempt to justify non-compliance with the then law of war by denying the existence of a state of war through some subterfuge such as labelling it a "police action," alleging the lack of a declaration of war, etc. Now, once again, it is necessary

7

to seek a method which will make it impossible for States to engage in armed conflict and attempt to justify non-compliance with the present (or future) law of armed conflict by advancing the same or new subterfuges, such as labelling the armed conflict as "legitimate self-defense," or as "assistance to an ally in an internal conflict," or as "assistance to peoples engaged in a national liberation movement aimed at throwing off the yoke of imperialism," etc.[41] And contriving new phrases of limitation will probably be no more successful in solving the problem than they have in the past as they would merely serve as a basis for future evasions of a different type.

It is suggested that a true and effective solution could be attained by assigning the power to make a determination as to the existence of a state of armed conflict to a pre-selected international body; by making the decision reached by that body as to the existence of a state of armed conflict binding on the States directly involved, as well as on all other Parties to the Convention; and by providing for the automatic imposition of total sanctions whenever this body determines that its decision is not being respected by a State party to the armed conflict in that such State has, despite such decision, continued to deny the applicability of the law of armed conflict, or any part of it, or is, in fact, violating such law.[42]

At the 1949 Diplomatic Conference two proposals were made which can be related to this problem. The Greek representative suggested that the existence of a state of belligerency should be decided by the Security Council of the United Nations. He later amplified this proposal by explaining that he had meant that such recognition of belligerency should be given by a majority of the countries represented on the Security Council.[43] A French proposal, which was actually concerned with the problem of a substitute for the Protecting Power, would have established on a permanent basis, immediately upon the Conventions becoming effective, a "High International Committee for the Protection of Humanity," consisting of thirty members elected by the Parties to the Convention from nominations made by the Parties, by the Hague "International [Permanent] Court of Arbitration," and by the "International Red Cross Standing Committee." Nominations were to be made from

> "amongst persons of high standing, without distinction of nationality, known for their moral authority, their spiritual and intellectual independence and the services they have rendered to humanity—

8

"In particular, they may be selected from amongst persons distinguished in the political, religious, scientific and legal domains, and amongst winners of the Nobel Peace Prize—"[44]

While this proposal was not incorporated into the Conventions, it was the subject of a resolution adopted by the Diplomatic Conference which recommended that consideration be given as soon as possible to the advisability of setting up an international body to perform the functions of a Protecting Power in the absence of such a Power.[45]

These two proposals are mentioned here because they suggest alternative methods of attempting to solve our problem: one by the use of an established political body; the other by the use of a new body created specifically for the purpose and which is made as neutral and apolitical as it is possible to do in these days of hypernationalism.

The suggested use of the Security Council (or, indeed, of any political body) is not considered to be a feasible solution. That body is composed of the representatives of States, voting on the basis of decisions reached in Foreign Offices, decisions which are made on the basis of self-interest and political expediency, and which are not necessarily consonant with the facts. It is inconceivable, for example, that the Security Council would ever reach a decision, over the opposition of North Vietnam (and, more important, of the Soviet Union), that the situation in Vietnam demands the application of the humanitarian conventions which govern the law of armed conflict.[46]

On the other hand, a specially constituted body of perhaps twenty-five individuals, each of whom is of sufficient personal international stature to be above politics and would act as an individual and as his or her moral and ethical principles dictated, detached and unaffected by instructions, could well constitute an acceptable and effective international body. The provisions for the selection of the members of this body (the "International Commission for the Enforcement of Humanitarian Rights during Armed Conflict"—ICEHRAC) would be sufficiently restrictive to ensure the choice of the type of individual described, without regard to nationality, race, religion, color, or geographical distribution. The ICEHRAC would be selected as soon as the constitutive convention had become effective and would be a permanent body, perhaps self-perpetuating.[47] Any Party to the convention, whether or not itself involved, could, at any time, request a determination by ICEHRAC as to whether the relationship between two or more States was such as to call into effect the application of the law of armed conflict; the States involved would be invited to present any facts or arguments they desired but would not otherwise participate in the decision-making process;[48] an affirmative decision would immediately be binding not only upon the States involved, but on all of the other Parties to the Convention; and a subsequent finding by ICEHRAC that its decision was not being complied with would automatically, and without further action of any kind, require the application of complete economic and communications sanctions against the violating State by all of the other Parties to the Convention.[49]

To many this proposal will undoubtedly appear Utopian, idealistic, and impractical. However, upon reflection this reaction may appear somewhat less valid. There are today more than one hundred States which are not presently involved in the type of armed conflict under discussion. Each and every one of them considers that should it become involved in such activities in the future, it would be on the side of the angels—so the provisions of any such convention would naturally apply in its favor and against the opponent. Moreover, to what will it have agreed? Merely that a neutral, internationally-created body, which it helped create, may determine that a situation in which that State unexpectedly finds itself calls for the application of the humanitarian law of armed conflict. What would that mean to it? Only that it could not kill, or otherwise maltreat, protected persons such as the sick and wounded, prisoners of war, and civilian noncombatants, and that it could not have recourse to certain prohibited methods of conducting hostilities. Can any State advance the argument that it refuses to ratify such a convention because it does not wish its sovereign power of action limited in these respects, it wishes to retain the unfettered ability to kill and maltreat these people at will and that it wishes, for example, to retain the possibility of using weapons which have been banned?[50] Moreover, once such a convention is drafted and presented for signature and ratification, the moral and humanitarian pressure to bring about ratifications would be tremendous and there would be an excellent possibility of its general acceptance.[51] While certain States which have adopted obsolete attitudes magnifying national sovereignty might well oppose such a proposal from beginning to end, it is predictable that they would participate, albeit reluctantly, in the diplomatic conference which was convened to draft such a convention and would eventually, rather than risk international opprobrium, become Parties to it.[52]

This, then, is the suggested remedy to the problem of establishing a method for the automatic determination that an existing situation necessitates the application of the law of armed conflict. While it would, it is true, entail a somewhat broader delegation of authority than States have heretofore been willing to make, it is believed that the time is past when States may argue "national sovereignty" as an excuse for refusing to participate in the creation of an international institution the sole function of which will be to limit the illegal and nonhumanitarian conduct of hostilities in armed conflict.

2. The non-existence of and the need for a method which will ensure the presence in the territory of each State party to an armed conflict of a Protecting Power or an international body with adequate authority to police compliance with that law.

Another major inadequacy in the old law of war and in the present law of armed conflict is that there has never been an "umpire" with sufficient authority to oversee the application of the law, to investigate alleged or possible violations, to determine the facts with respect thereto, and to take the necessary action to ensure the correction of the default.

For many centuries there has existed in customary international law an institution known as the Protecting Power. By the time of the Spanish-American War (1898), the traditional functions of that Protecting Power had come to include some aspects of the protection of prisoners of war.[53] During World War I a number of formal agreements were entered into confirming the existence of the Protecting Power and its activities with respect to prisoners of war, which had until then rested entirely on custom, and specifying a number of functions.[54] Subsequently, in Article 86 of the 1929 Geneva Prisoner-of-War Convention[55] this institution received formal recognition in a general multilateral treaty concerned with ensuring humanitarian treatment for one class of victims of war.

The four 1949 Geneva Conventions reaffirm the Protecting Power as an international humanitarian institution.[56] There is now, therefore, binding international legislation establishing the Protecting Power as an international institution during time of armed conflict and specifying a number of its duties and powers with respect to the protection of wounded and sick, prisoners of war, and civilian noncombatants. Unfortunately, the provision concerning the original designation of Protecting Powers by belligerents is less than clear, apparently relying on customary international law in this respect, although a great deal of time, effort, and controversy were expended at the 1949 Diplomatic Conference with respect to the designation of replacements and substitutes for an original Protecting Power.[57] In any event, although there have probably been close to one hundred armed conflicts of various sorts and sizes since the end of World War II, the institution of the Protecting Power has not once during that period been called into being.[58] While the Report advances a number of possible reasons for this failure,[59] it is believed that many of them are completely irrelevant and that, for the most part, the failure to secure the designation of such a Power has resulted from the fact that the States involved did not wish to have on their territory a neutral presence concerned with the problem of the extent to which there was compliance with the provisions of the specifically humanitarian conventions governing the law of armed conflict.[60]

The failure of the Protecting Power as an institution and the need for some effective system of supervision appears to be very generally admitted. Thus in answer to the Secretary-General's inquiry concerning the preparation of his Report, India stated that it believed that the solution to the problem "would perhaps be found more through the complete implementation of the existing conventions than through the search for new legal instruments."[61] And the response of the United States acknowledged "a strongly held conviction that steps are urgently needed to secure better application of existing humanitarian international conventions to armed conflicts."[62] Similarly, the Report states that

> "there would be pressing need for measures to improve and strengthen the present system of international supervision and assistance to parties to armed conflicts in their observance of humanitarian norms of international law. . . ."[63]

And another organization concerned with preserving humanitarian rights said, with respect to the Protecting Power:

12

"Certainly it is time that this valuable international custom was revived in the modern context of armed conflicts. An initiative of this kind by the United Nations would set a precedent as a means of lessening the brutality of conflicts, and would accord with the aim expressed in the Charter. . . ."[64]

And, finally, Resolution XI of the XXIst International Conference of the Red Cross "calls upon all parties to allow the Protecting Power or the International Committee of the Red Cross free access to prisoners of war and to all places of their detention."[65] Further, it should be borne in mind that nowhere in either customary or conventional international law is there any rule which would authorize the Protecting Power, even if it were designated and functioning, to supervise the compliance of a belligerent with that area of the law of armed conflict governing the conduct of hostilities.[66]

Although, as has been stated, no Protecting Power has been designated in any armed conflict which has occurred since World War II, on a number of occasions the ICRC has been permitted to perform its humanitarian functions.[67] Perhaps because of this, the Report calls it the most effective private organization concerned with respect for human rights in armed conflict, ascribes this to "its history, past experience, and its established and well deserved reputation of impartiality," and recommends its strengthening.[68] But not even the ICRC has been uniformly successful in having its services accepted. Thus while it was permitted to perform humanitarian functions in the prisoner-of-war camps maintained in South Korea during the period of hostilities in that country (1950-53), it was never permitted in North Korea where, as a result, there was no "guardian" of the Conventions;[69] similarly, while it has functioned in South Vietnam over a considerable period of time, it has never been permitted in North Vietnam;[70] and its trials and tribulations in Biafra and Nigeria are too recent to require elaboration.[71]

There is, then, a double need in this area: (1) a need to devise a method which will ensure the existence of a "third" presence, either a Protecting Power or some substitute therefor, on the territory of each State party to an armed conflict; and (2) a need to grant to that Protecting Power, or the substitute therefor, adequate authority to ensure compliance with all of the law of armed conflict, including that relating to the conduct of hostilities.[72] The provisions of the 1949 Geneva Conventions for the

13

designation of Protecting Powers have not been at all effective[73] and those relating to substitutes for Protecting Powers have been only partially successful. It is apparent, then, that the only real solution would be, once again, to have a provision in a convention which would, in appropriate cases, automatically trigger action by ICEHRAC.[74] Thus the convention creating that institution could provide that, when the existence of a state of armed conflict is acknowledged by the States involved, or when a decision to that effect has been reached by ICEHRAC in accordance with the other provisions of the convention, and no Protecting Powers have been designated in accordance with customary international law[75] within one week thereafter, ICEHRAC would automatically begin to function in the capacity of a substitute for the Protecting Power, with all the rights and duties which have been, or which may be, granted to such Powers.[76] And such rights and duties should include the supervision of the application of *all* of the law of armed conflict and should not be restricted to the protections afforded under the 1949 Geneva Conventions. After all, a human being, combatant or noncombatant, suffers just as much, or is just as dead, be his improper treatment due to a violation of those conventions or to the use of dum-dum bullets (in violation of the 1899 Hague Declaration), or the use of poison (in violation of the 1907 Hague Regulations), or the use of gas (in violation of the 1925 Geneva Protocol), etc.[77]

In many respects the foregoing proposal parallels suggestions contained in the Report.[78] Nor is it believed that the U.S.S.R. and the other Communist countries would necessarily oppose such a solution merely because they made reservations to Article 10/10/10/11,[79] and because the Soviet Union made a statement indicating that it did not consider Resolution 2 of the 1949 Diplomatic Conference necessary.[80] Events subsequent to 1949 have demonstrated the need for an institution capable of performing the functions of the Protecting Power and competent to take such functions upon itself immediately the need therefor becomes apparent.[81] It is believed that only in this fashion will the world community of nations provide a satisfactory and effective method of ensuring in every case of armed conflict the presence of an impartial agency with the function of making certain that the law of armed conflict is fully and properly applied.[82]

14

3. The non-existence of and the need for a complete and total prohibition of the use in armed conflict of any and all categories of chemical and biological agents.

A third major inadequacy in the existing law relating to the protection of individuals during armed conflict is the lack of a comprehensive and generally accepted ban on the use as weapons of all types and categories of both chemical and biological agents.

While there is probably no real equal to the disaster that would descend upon this earth should an all-out nuclear war occur, potentially the use of other uncontrollable methods of mass destruction could be almost equally disastrous for mankind.[83] Dozens of chemical agents, and numerous biological agents,[84] all with varying degrees of lethality, have been determined to be the most "useful" are now included in the arsenals of a number of nations for possible use in the event of armed conflict.[85] Hundreds of books and articles have been written[86] and millions of words have been spoken[87] on the subject. For the most part they have been concerned with the questions of whether there is today any customary rule of international law which prohibits the use of chemical agents in armed conflict and whether biological agents fall within the well-established prohibitions against the use of "poisons" and against the use of weapons which cause "unnecessary suffering"; but also, in more recent days, with the inhumanity of these weapons and the highlighting of the moral and ethical basis for the universal acceptance by nations of a strict and all-inclusive ban on the use in armed conflict of any and all types of both chemical and biological agents.[88]

A very brief history of the attempts to ban the use of chemical (and bacteriological) agents as weapons will probably serve to clarify the current problem as well as the suggestion for solving it. Chemical warfare of differing varieties has existed for centuries.[89] Although the 1868 Declaration of St. Petersburg[90] actually dealt with explosive bullets, it is often cited as the beginning of the attempt to ban the use of chemical agents in armed conflict because of a preambular clause which deplored "the employment of arms which uselessly aggravate the suffering of disabled men, or render their death inevitable." Chemical agents, it is contended, fall within this classification.

The 1899 Hague Peace Conference adopted a number of provisions which are said to have indirectly, or which did directly, ban the use of chemical agents. Thus the Regulations attached to the

15

Second Hague Convention[91] drafted by that Conference stated that the right of belligerents to adopt means of injuring the enemy was not unlimited (Art. 22) and they especially prohibited the employment of poison or poisoned weapons (Art. 23a) and of arms, projectiles, or material of a nature to cause unnecessary suffering (Art. 23e). In addition, a Declaration concerning the Prohibition of Using Projectiles the Sole Object of which is the Diffusion of Asphyxiating or Deleterious Gases was drafted.[92] While this Declaration was not repeated at the 1907 Hague Peace Conference, the provisions of the Regulations attached to the Fourth Hague Convention of 1907[93] were identical with those cited from its 1899 predecessor.

World War I saw the use of gas introduced by Germany, followed thereafter by its use by the Allies. The Treaty of Versailles contained an article which stated that the "use of asphyxiating, poisonous or other gases and all analogous liquids, materials or devices being prohibited, their manufacture and importation are strictly forbidden in Germany."[94] Nevertheless, it would be an exaggeration to say that when the Treaty of Versailles was signed in 1919 there was in existence any generally accepted rule of international law prohibiting the use of chemical agents in armed conflict. In 1922 the five great maritime nations of that time (France, Italy, Japan, the United Kingdom, and the United States) drafted and signed the Treaty of Washington relating to the use of submarines and noxious gases which contained a provision that the use of "asphyxiating, poisonous or other gases, and all analogous liquids, materials or devices, having been justly condemned by the general opinion of the civilized world and a prohibition of such use having been declared in treaties to which a majority of the civilized Powers are parties," the signatories "declare their assent to such prohibition."[95] While this treaty never became effective (France failed to ratify it because of the provisions relating to submarines), it constituted an important landmark in the law of armed conflict. And three years later, at the Conference which met in Geneva to establish controls on international trade in munitions,[96] a Protocol was drafted which contained wording lifted bodily from the Treaty of Washington and, in addition, contained an agreement "to extend this prohibition to the use of bacteriological methods of warfare."[97] As of October 30, 1969, there were 68 States parties to this 1925 Geneva Protocol.[98] The great majority, however, have ratified it with reservations which make it

16

applicable only as regards other States which are also Parties to it; and which make it inapplicable in the event it is violated by the enemy.[99]

Gas was subsequently used by Italy against Ethiopia in the 1935-36 war.[100] Italy admitted this use in the League of Nations and unsuccessfully attempted to justify it as a reprisal for other alleged violations of international law by Ethiopia. Japan used gas against China in their hostilities of the late 1930s; and the Soviet Union contended that Japan used bacteriological agents against China in the 1930s. This was never established by acceptable evidence and, so far as appears, there was no use in armed conflict of either chemical or bacteriological weapons by any belligerent during World War II.[101] During the Korean hostilities the Soviet Union, Communist China, and North Korea all contended that the United States forces in the United Nations Command had used bacteriological weapons.[102] The United States denied this and demanded an investigation which was refused. It is interesting to note that in an official book published in Moscow in 1967 no mention is made of these allegations, although the charge against the Japanese is reiterated and the use of defoliants in Vietnam is strongly criticized.[103] The charge was also made, and apparently verified by the ICRC, that Egypt used a chemical agent against the Royalists in the Yemen.[104] Egypt denied the charge and invited an investigation. As in the case of the similar demand made by the United States in Korea, no such investigation ever took place.

demanded an investigation which was refused. It is interesting to note that in an official book published in Moscow in 1967 no mention is made of these allegations, although the charge against the Japanese is reiterated and the use of defoliants in Vietnam is strongly criticized.[103] The charge was also made, and apparently verified by the ICRC, that Egypt used a chemical agent against the Royalists in the Yemen.[104] Egypt denied the charge and invited an investigation. As in the case of the similar demand made by the United States in Korea, no such investigation ever took place.

The ICRC Draft Rules contain a blunt and broad prohibition against the use of "incendiary, chemical, bacteriological, radioactive or other agents";[105] on a number of occasions the General Assembly has adopted resolutions calling for strict observance of the "principles and objectives" of the 1925 Geneva Protocol and inviting non-Parties to accede to it;[106] and on at least one occasion it has declared the use of chemical and biological agents of warfare "as contrary to the generally recognized rules of international law, as embodied in the Protocol."[107] Some writers also urge that the use of these weapons is prohibited by customary international law.[108] It appears however that, particularly in the light of recent developments, this is a sterile approach to the problem.

When the 1925 Geneva Protocol was sent to the United States Senate for its advice and consent to ratification, this was refused; and accordingly, the United States is not presently a Party to the Protocol.[109] As a result, the United States has long taken the position that, while it will not be the first user of the weapons prohibited by that international agreement, it "is not a party to any treaty, now in force, that prohibits or restricts the use in warfare of toxic or nontoxic gases, of smoke or incendiary materials, or of bacteriological warfare." [110] Although the United States has not used any toxic chemical, or any bacteriological agent, since the Protocol became effective as between the Parties to it, the fact that it refused to ratify the Protocol has not only caused it to have problems in the diplomatic field,[111] but has also undoubtedly deterred a number of other States from becoming Parties to it.

On November 25, 1969, President Nixon made an announcement of major importance concerning this subject.[112] This announcement included:

1. A reaffirmation of the renunciation by the United States of the first use of lethal chemical weapons;

2. An extension of this renunciation to the first use of incapacitating chemicals;

3. An intention to resubmit the 1925 Geneva Protocol to the Senate for its advice and consent to ratification;

4. Renunciation by the United States of the use of lethal biological agents and weapons;

5. Confining biological research to defense measures;

6. Disposing of all stocks of bacteriological weapons; and

7. Associating the United States with the principles and objectives of the United Kingdom Draft Convention on biological weapons.[113]

It is assumed that this action by the United States, its prospective ratification of the 1925 Geneva Protocol, and its expressed willingness to become a party to a convention banning biologicals will lead the way to the goal which the United Nations General Assembly has long sought to reach—universal acceptance of prohibitions on chemical and biological agents and weapons.[114] Unfortunately, it appears that there is still one major problem which requires solution—the status of the use of certain types of chemical agents. For while diplomats, scientists, and international lawyers are, for the most part, in general agreement that lethal gases and all biologicals either are, or should be, prohibited by the law of armed conflict, there is no such concordance with respect to: the so-called non-lethal gases, such as tear gas (CS); incendiaries, such as napalm; and defoliants. Moreover, the use of all of these weapons by the United States in Vietnam has considerably exacerbated this problem.

The difference of opinion with respect to both the legal and the moral aspects of the problem of the use of non-lethal or incapacitating chemicals such as tear gas (lachrymatories) is evidenced by the division among the group of experts convened by the ICRC:

". . . Some [experts] . . . wondered whether the employment against the enemy of chemical agents involving no serious danger for health might not in the final issue be of a more humanitarian character than many other means of warfare. The employment of means such as police gases (lachrymatory and others) is admitted on the national level: why could they not a fortiori be admitted against the enemy?

"Other experts, on the contrary, considered that the prohibition in the 1925 Geneva Protocol should be taken as covering *all gases,* including those not directly poisonous, in virtue of the deliberately broad terms of this prohibition in the Protocol . . ."[115]

In 1930 the United Kingdom took the position that the use of smoke did not violate the Protocol but that the use of tear gas did; but recently a spokesman for that country stated that today's tear gas is less harmful to man than was the 1930 smoke; that it is used widely for domestic purposes for riot control; and that its use is not prohibited by any international convention.[116]

Apart from the fact that even a non-lethal, incapacitating gas will occasionally cause a fatality, there are two major objections voiced against their use in armed conflict: first, that as a practical matter the legality of their use becomes extremely debatable when

19

its purpose is "to enhance the effectiveness of conventional weapons,"[117] "to force persons from protective covering to face attack by fragmentation bombs"; and second, and more important, that the use of any chemical, albeit non-lethal, results inevitably in escalation: "except perhaps when they are first used, non-lethal chemical weapons are unlikely to have much effect except to set the stage for more deadly CBW operations."[119]

The second chemical weapon in the controversial area is napalm—an extremely effective weapon and hence one which is much feared,[120] and much denounced.[121] Once again there is no general agreement as to whether this chemical weapon is prohibited by the Protocol.[122] And because the answer to this question is even more difficult to ascertain than is that with respect to lachrymatories, the position has been taken that it may be used, but only in a discriminating manner.[123] The suggestion is made in A/7720 that in measures of control and disarmament incendiary weapons such as napalm should be considered separately from chemical and biological weapons and that a new convention is needed to clarify the situation;[124] a suggestion which is probably an admission that this is presently a gray area of the law.

Prior to Vietnam defoliants had never been used in warfare. As a result, there is no real experience upon which scientists can base their opinions as to the ecological effects of their use.[125] Here, as in the case of napalm, the suggestion has been made that the legality of their use depends upon the purpose or target: while it might be permissible to use them on a forest area used by combat troops, it would not be permissible to use them on farm lands raising crops to feed the civilian population. Apart from the fact that it would frequently be all but impossible to make the correct determinations, if the use of defoliants does change the ecology, then it would appear that the purpose or target should not be the determining factor in reaching a decision on their use.[126]

Because the use of non-lethal, or incapacitating, chemical agents will inevitably lead to the use of other, more lethal, chemical agents; because napalm can cause both asphyxiation and unnecessary suffering; because defoliants may well change the entire ecology of an area and could lead to the starvartion of the civilian population; because of these and many other reasons, it is believed that to be successful any prohibition on the use of chemical weapons in armed conflict must comprise *all* types of chemical agents, including those just mentioned. It is on this basis that it is urged that there is a vital humanitarian need for a universally accepted understanding that the prohibition of the use in armed conflict of chemical agents includes any and all categories of such agents, not excluding incapacitating gases, incendiaries, and defoliants.[127]

There is comparatively little dispute on the need for a far-reaching prohibition on the use of biologicals in armed conflict. As has been noted, there is general agreement that, like a nuclear war, a biological war would constitute a disaster to all mankind, belligerent and neutral, combatant and noncombatant.[128] One grave problem in this area is that even a small, comparatively undeveloped nation could conceivably mass the necessary resources to enter this field—and there is considerable dispute as to whether an inspection system, even if adopted, could function effectively.[129] The United Kingdom Draft Convention on the subject of biological weapons does not provide for inspections except in the context of a specific complaint.[130] But, while every effort should most certainly be made to devise means of ensuring against the illegal production and storage of biological agents of military relevance by any nation, large or small, industrial or undeveloped, this should not be permitted to unduly delay agreement on a treaty completely outlawing the use in armed conflict of any and all biological agents.

4. *The non-existence of and the need for a complete code governing the use of air power in armed conflict with emphasis on the outright prohibition of any type of bombing which has as its basic target the civilian population.*

The airplane was first successfully flown in 1903, just shortly prior to the Second Hague Conference of 1907; it developed into a military weapon of sizable proportions during World War I; during the between-wars period it became obvious that it was a major military weapon; during and since World War II technological advances in this field have been such that its importance in the military arsenal is now unequalled (except for the nuclear ballistic missile); and yet its use in armed conflict remains essentially unregulated!

In 1917, while the airplane was still in swaddling clothes, exponents of the use of air power had already evolved the theory that

21

"the day may not be far off when aerial operations with their devastation of enemy lands and destruction of industrial and populous centres on a vast scale may become the principal operations of war."[131]

While strategic bombing was probably not the "principal operation" of World War II, it certainly played a most important role in that war and will do so again in any future non-nuclear armed conflict—and perhaps even in one involving the use of nuclear weapons.[132]

As in the case of the discussion of chemical and biological weapons, while it is unproductive to argue about whether or not the strategic bombing of World War II violated international law,[133] a brief survey of what has transpired in the past will prove helpful in approaching the problem from the point of view of the future. When the Second Hague Peace Conference met in 1907 the balloon was more than a century old and had already been used for military purposes, while the airplane had been successfully flown for the first time only four years before. The Conference adopted a Declaration prohibiting bombing "from balloons or by other new methods of a similar nature"[134] and Conventions which included restrictions on land bombardment and naval bombardment. Article 25 of the Regulations on the Laws and Customs of War[135] provided:

"The attack or bombardment *by whatever means,* of towns, villages, dwellings, or buildings which are undefended is prohibited." (Emphasis added.)

The records of the Conference indicate that the words "by whatever means" were included in the article in order to cover air bombardment.[136] And Article 2 of the Convention on Naval Bombardment[137] excluded from the prohibition against the bombing of undefended places "military works, military or naval establishments, depots of arms or war materiel, workshops or plants which could be utilized for the needs of the hostile fleet or army." The argument has been advanced, not without justification, that this provision provides a basis for the air bombardment in the "hinterland" of objectives such as those enumerated.

This was the extent of the efforts which had been made to control the use of air power when World War I began; and during its course the airplane became a full-fledged weapon. However,

22

apart from a few incidents its use was restricted to the battlefield and, usually, to air-to-air duels.[138] In view of the technological progress made and foreseen, it is indeed strange that although a number of efforts were made in the between-wars period to obtain an international agreement on such matters as air bombardment, none was successful.[139] The most authoritative of these failures was the drafting of the 1923 Hague Rules of Air Warfare.[140] Two articles of those Rules are particularly relevant: Article 22, which would have prohibited aerial bombardment which was "for the purpose of terrorizing the civilian population . . . or of injuring noncombatants"; and Article 24, which would have limited it to specified military objectives in the vicinity of the zone of land operations and then only if it would result in a distinct military advantage and if it could be accomplished without "indiscriminate" bombing of the civilian population. These two articles were intended: (1) to preserve the traditional distinction between combatant and noncombatant; and (2) to limit the allowable military objectives to those in the area of the combat zone—the so-called "occupation bombardment" because it is normally preliminary to physical occupation.

In a discussion of air bombardment in the House of Commons on June 21, 1938, Prime Minister Chamberlain made the following statement:

"I think we may say that there are, at any rate, three rules of international law or three principles of international law which are as applicable to warfare from the air as they are to war at sea or on land. In the first place, it is against international law to bomb civilians as such and to make deliberate attacks upon civilian populations. That is undoubtedly a violation of international law. In the second place, targets which are aimed at from the air must be legitimate military objectives and must be capable of identification. In the third place, reasonable care must be taken in attacking these military objectives so that by carelessness a civilian population in the neighborhood is not bombed."[141]

When World War II erupted in September 1939, President Roosevelt immediately sent the belligerents a plea against the bombing of civilian populations. The British, French, and Germans all replied that their planes were instructed to attack military objectives only.[142] In March 1940 the ICRC made an appeal to the belligerents "to confirm general immunity for peaceful populations, to define their military objectives, and to refrain from indiscriminate bombardments and reprisals." Once again the belligerents responded affirmatively—but continued to act as they felt necessary.[143] The estimate has been made that while World War I caused 10 million deaths, of which 500,000 were civilians, World War II caused 50 million, of which 24 million were civilians; and that half of the civilian deaths (12 million) were caused by air raids![144] It is worthy of note, too, that such air attacks were not specifically included in the definition of war crimes in the Charter of the International Military Tribunal and that there were no post-war trials based on a charge of indiscriminate bombardment of the civilian population.[145] Nevertheless, Spaight takes the position that "nothing that has happened in the second world war has shaken the legal objection to indiscriminate bombing."[146]

It is apparent from the foregoing that the attempt to control aerial bombardment juridically has been based on analogy to two classical principles of land and sea warfare: (1) the distinction between combatant and noncombatant; and (2) the restricting of lawful targets to military objectives.[147]

Much of the humanitarian law regulating armed conflict which has been accepted during the past century has been based upon the distinction between combatant and noncombatant. The airman who has crashed and been hospitalized, the sailor who has been rescued from the sea by the enemy after his ship has been sunk, the soldier who has been captured on the field of battle—all of these have been removed from combatant status and are therefore entitled to the humanitarian protection afforded by international law. But they are but a comparatively small percentage of the overall group of noncombatants, the vast majority of whom are simply civilians, persons who are not a part of the armed forces of a belligerent. It is with these latter that we are presently concerned. The distinction between combatant and civilian has been termed, and properly so, "the fundamental principle of the law of war."[148] But air warfare in general, and strategic bombing in particular, has tended to blur that distinction[149] and its validity has been questioned.[150]

Let us take three examples. First, a city of 500,000 population located in the "hinterland" (deep inside the country and far from the scene of actual land combat) has no factories making any product in support of the country's war effort. Is the city a proper target for air bombardment? Second, suppose that this same city

24

has in its midst a factory employing 1000 workers making a very important instrument of war. Is the factory, or the city, a proper target for air bombardment? And third, suppose that the same city has within its area a number of factories making important instruments of war, and employing the entire work force of the city. Are the factories, or is the city, a proper target for air bombardment?

Under the classical rules discussed and enumerated above, to bomb the city with no war production factories would be terror bombing, pure and simple, and would be a violation of the law of armed conflict. It would be an attack on a non-military objective which could be of no military advantage to the attacker except the possible demoralization of the enemy civilian population. With respect to this type of activity Lauterpacht has said:

> ". . . it is in that prohibition, which is a clear rule of law, of intentional terrorization—or destruction—of the civilian population as an avowed or obvious object of attack that lies the last vestige of the claim that war can be legally regulated at all. Without that irreducible principle of restraint there is no limit to the license and depravity of force. . . ."[151]

Even the proponents of more "liberal" rules of air bombardment do not assert the legality of bombing of this type.[152]

What of the large city with only one small factory in which is made a product of value to its country's war-effort? Certainly the bombing and destruction of such a factory would meet the test of resulting in a distinct military advantage to the attacker. It would not meet the test of being located in the zone of operations—but is that test, originally established when only cities in the zone of land operations could be reached by artillery bombardment, a valid test to be applied to air bombardment which can reach anywhere in the world? Moreover, it would meet the test of the requirements for naval bombardment. It would probably not meet the test of being located where the bombing can take place without danger to the civilian population. However, it appears that practice during and since World War II would permit the factory to be subjected to air attack. As the Report points out, in recent armed conflicts belligerents have frequently made accusations of attacks upon non-military objectives and the enemy belligerent has denied the fact without either side questioning the propriety of the distinciton as to types of objectives.[153]

Finally, what of the large city with many factories and most of the work force engaged in the war effort? Let us assume that in time of armed conflict 40% of the population constitute the work force—but that still means that 60% of the civilian population, 300,000 people of this city, is made up of women, children, aged, sick, etc. Must the attacker pick out individual targets, the real military objectives? Or may he blanket the entire city with bombs, thus ensuring that all of the plants are destroyed—but also ensuring that a large part of the population, worker and nonworker, is likewise destroyed? Spaight would answer this latter question in the affirmative. He says:

> ". . . There are in any given enemy city thousands of civilians; of 'noncombatants' in the old sense, but there are also thousands who cannot be called 'noncombatants' in any true meaning of the term. The former suffer inevitably because the latter have, quite properly, to be prevented from pursuing their lethal activities. It is a tragedy of juxtaposition which is not entirely without precedent. Noncombatants have often suffered in bombardments by land and naval forces, but their suffering has never been held to make the bombardment illegal. . . ."[154]

And he repeatedly asserts that so-called "target-area bombing" is an "established usage" and that it "cannot be considered to offend against the principles of the international law of war."[155] The problem which then confronts us is that we have returned to the doctrine of "total war,"[156] war as fought centuries ago: when the besieged city fell, all of its inhabitants were slaughtered and the city itself was put to the torch.

The Report makes the suggestion with respect to strategic bombing conducted on a target-area basis that "(it) would seem that measures to examine the effects of this kind of military operations within their legal context may now be desirable, and the question of defining limits might be usefully studied."[157] With this modest proposal there can be no possible dispute. The question which then presents itself is, what are possible solutions to the problem? And, which of these possible solutions offers the greatest amount of protection to the civilian population? [158]

Air bombardment could, of course, be limited to areas where combat is actually taking place—the old concept of the "zone of operations." This, in effect, means tactical bombing, and would preclude strategic bombing. While this would, in large part, solve the problem, it is extremely doubtful that it would be possible to secure the agreement of Governments to such a stringent rule. Moreover, even if the agreement of Governments were obtained, it is doubtful that there would be compliance with such a rule in practice.

The Report proposes the establishment of safety zones,[159] apparently similar to, but much larger than, the hospital zones referred to in Annex I to the First and Fourth Geneva Conventions of 1949.[160] Presumably there would be no bombing whatsoever permitted within the safety zones and no restrictions on bombing elsewhere. While this might work for small groups and in small areas, it appears to be totally impractical for the protection of tens or hundreds of millions of civilians. The logistic problem alone would be insurmountable; and with thousands of square miles within a safety zone, the unlawful use of such areas for the protection of important military matters would probably be inevitable.

The Draft Rules prepared by the ICRC and submitted to the XIXth International Conference of the Red Cross at New Delhi in 1957[161] contain a number of provisions intended to provide maximum protection for the civilian population. An examination of the various provisions of these Draft Rules makes it clear why they were received by the Governments with a "crushing silence." While they are, as would be expected, as humanitarian as it would be possible to draft such rules, they are also impractical to the point where it is extremely doubtful that any armed force would be able to comply with them in time of armed conflict. While this, as we shall see, is not true of all of these Draft Rules, a much more practical set of general principles was drafted by the ICRC for consideration by its group of experts in 1968. These principles would limit air bombardment to identified military objectives; would place upon the attacker the duty to use care in attacking the identified military objective; and would apply the principle of proportionality as between the identified military objective and any possible harm to the civilian population.[162] These principles would clearly prohibit target-area bombing; but there does not appear to be any reason why such an important rule should not be specifically set out.

It is clear now, as it has been in the past, that no rule has as yet been conceived which will give full protection to the civilian

27

population and yet will be acceptable to Governments. However, if man can devise instruments to send a spaceship to the moon and have it land within a matter of yards from its target, man can certainly devise, if he has not already done so, instruments which will put a bomb exactly on target. On the basis of this premise, the following rules on aerial bombardment are suggested:

1. *Terror Bombing Prohibited.* Attacks directed against the civilian population, as such, whether with the object of terrorizing it, or for any other reason, are prohibited.[163]

2. *Target-Area Bombing Prohibited.* It is forbidden to attack, as a single objective, an area including several military objectives at a distance from one another where members of the civilian population are located between such military objectives.[164]

3. *Military Objectives.*
- (a) Before bombing a military objective, the attacking force must have sufficiently identified it as such.[165]
- (b) In bombardments against military objectives, the attacking force must take every possible precaution in order to avoid inflicting damage on the civilian population.[166]
- (c) To constitute a military objective a target must fall within one of the categories listed in the annex hereto.[167]

It is believed that these rules will, under present and foreseeable technological standards, provide a maximum of protection to the civilian population, while placing acceptable limitations on the scope of strategic bombing.

Conclusion

Armed conflict is, by its very nature, unhumanitarian. However, humanitarian rules, properly applied, can do much to mitigate this situation. It is believed that were the proposals made herein to be adopted as part of the law of armed conflict, they would go far to provide additional needed protection for both combatant and civilian noncombatant.

As has been stated, this paper represents an attempt to deal with only *some* of the present major inadequacies of the law of armed conflict; and their selection and priority must be ascribed to the personal predilections of the author. There are a number of other areas which might well have been included and which may well be considered by some to have equal, or even greater, importance. These might include: enforcement of the law of armed conflict; combat at sea, particularly submarine warfare; the status of guerrillas and partisans; the use of starvation as a weapon; etc. The selection made of the subjects to be discussed should certainly not be considered as in any way denigrating the importance to the cause of humanitarianism in armed conflict of many other such subjects.

APPENDIX 1

Twenty-third session
Agenda item 62

RESOLUTION ADOPTED BY THE
GENERAL ASSEMBLY

[on the report of the Third Committee (A/7433)]

2444 (XXIII). *Respect for human rights in armed conflicts*

The General Assembly,
Recognizing the necessity of applying basic humanitarian principles in all armed conflicts,
Taking note of resolution XXIII on human rights in armed conflicts, adopted on 12 May 1968 by the International Conference on Human Rights,[1]
Affirming that the provisions of that resolution need to be implemented as soon as possible,

1. *Affirms* resolution XXVIII of the XXth International Conference of the Red Cross held at Vienna in 1965, which laid down, *inter alia,* the following principles for observance by all governmental and other authorities responsible for action in armed conflicts:
(a) That the right of the parties to a conflict to adopt means of injuring the enemy is not unlimited;
(b) That it is prohibited to launch attacks against the civilian population as such;
(c) That distinction must be made at all times between persons taking part in the hostilities and members of the civilian population to the effect that the latter be spared as much as possible;

2. *Invites* the Secretary-General, in consultation with the International Committee of the Red Cross and other appropriate international organizations, to study:
(a) Steps which could be taken to secure the better application of existing humanitarian international conventions and rules in all armed conflicts;
(b) The need for additional humanitarian international conventions or for other appropriate legal instruments to ensure the better protection of civilians, prisoners and combatants in all armed conflicts and the prohibition and limitation of the use of certain methods and means of warfare;

3. *Requests* the Secretary-General to take all other necessary steps to give effect to the provisions of the present resolution and to report to the General Assembly at its twenty-fourth session on the steps he has taken;

4. *Further requests* Member States to extend all possible assistance to the

31

Secretary-General in the preparation of the study requested in paragraph 2 above;

5. *Calls upon* all States which have not done so to become parties to the Hague Convention of 1899 and 1907,[2] the Geneva Protocol of 1925[3] and the Geneva Conventions of 1949.[4]

1748th plenary meeting,
19 December 1968.

FOOTNOTES

[1] See *Final Act of the International Conference on Human Rights* (United Nations publication, Sales No.: E. 68. XIV. 2), p. 18.

[2] Carnegie Endowment for International Peace, *The Haue Convention and Declarations 1899-1907* (New York: Oxford University Press, 1918).

[3] League of Nations, *Treaty Series,* vol. XCIV (1929), No. 2138.

[4] United Nations, *Treaty Series,* vol. 75 (1950), Nos. 970-973.

[1] Stone, Legal Controls of International Conflict 335 (1954, reprinted 1959). The statement that the codified law of war still exceeds the law of peace is probably now no longer true in view of the perhaps unanticipated success of the International Law Commission in securing the acceptance of a number of its draft conventions such as those on the Law of the Sea, Diplomatic Immunities, Consular Relations, and Treaties.

[2] See note 84 *infra.* To a limited extent it might be considered that the 1954 Hague Convention for the Protection of Cultural property in the Event of Armed Conflict (249 U.N.T.S. 215) also falls in this category; but, of course, it attempts to protect property, not people.

[3] International Committee of the Red Cross, Reaffirmation and Development of the Laws and Customs Applicable in Armed Conflict 6 (1969) [hereinafter cited as ICRC, Reaffirmation]. This document is a report submitted to the XXIst International Conference of the Red Cross, held in Istanbul in September 1969.

[4] It has at times been suggested that the condition for the termination of the 1907 Hague Declaration Prohibiting the Discharge of Projectiles and Explosives from Balloons (36 Stat. 2439; 2 Am. J. Int'l L. Supp. 216 (1908)) has never occurred and that, therefore, the Declaration is still in force. In view of the practice of nations prior to, during, and since World War II, there would appear to be little merit to such an argument. Moreover, the United States and the United Kingdom are the only major powers which ratified it.

[5] "The League of Nations and the Laws of War," 1920-21 Brit. Ybk. Int'l L. 109, 114-15.

[6] Ray, Commentaire du Pacte de la Société des Nations 528 (1930).

[7] Constantopoulos, "Les raisons de la crise du droit de la guerre," 7 Jahrbuch für Internationales Recht 22, 25 (1957). In this regard, see note 11 *infra.*

[8] Writing in 1931 one author pointed out that neither the Pact of the League of Nations, nor the Kellogg-Briand Pact of 1928, could *guarantee* that there would be no future wars. Rasmussen, Code des Prisonniers de Guerre 72 (1931). And commenting on the 1934 Monaco Conference, de la Pradelle said:

> ". . . Doctors and lawyers denounced the conspiracy of silence which, lest public opinion be frightened, had been adopted in official circles and which consisted of not speaking about the laws of war." (Translation mine.)

La Conférence Diplomatique et les Nouvelles Conventions de Genève du 12 aout 1949, at 13 (1951).

[9] 36 Stat. 2277; 2 Am. J. INT'l L. Supp. 90 (1908).

[10] It is true that occasional attempts to further codify some limited aspects of the law of war were made, despite the inhospitable atmosphere. Thus, naval conferences were held in Washington in 1922 and in London in

1930 and 1936. However, these conferences, which were not even always successful in producing an effective result, merely scratched the surface of the work which needed to be done.

[11] It is essential to bear in mind that to a considerable extent the existing law of war *was* observed during World War II. True, there were many well publicized violations of that law, the so-called "conventional war crimes." But see Baxter, "The Role of Law in Modern War," 1953 Proc. Am. Soc. Int'l L. 90, 92 where the following appears:

> "Those who are most scornful of the attempts which the law of war makes to mitigate human suffering in war inevitably point to the barbarities which were practiced in the second World War. These accusations overlook the extent to which states did comply with the law of war, the advantage of a fixed standard against which to measure the conduct of those who were the most flagrant in the violation of all international law, and the subsequent vindication of the validity of the norms of international law through the imposition of sanctions in the war crimes proceedings. . . ."

[12] Report of the International Law Commission to the General Assembly on the Work of the First Session, 1949 Ykb. Int'l L. Comm'n 281. And the International Law Commission did not stand alone. See, for example, the position of Scelle, set forth in Francois, "Réconsideration des principes du droit de la guerre," 47 (I) Annuaire de l'Institut de Droit International 491, 493 (1957); and Fenwick's comment on Baxter, "Forces for Compliance with the Law of War," 1964 Proc. Am. Soc. Int'l L. 82, 97.

[13] See, for example, Kunz, "The Chaotic Status of the Laws of War and the Urgent Necessity for their Revision," 45 Am. J. Int'l L. 37 (1951); Lauterpacht, "The Problem of the Revision of the Law of War," 29 Brit. Ykb. Int'l L. 360 (1952); Coudert, Francois and Lauterpacht, "La revision du droit de la guerre," 45 (I) Annuaire de l'Institut de Droit International 555 (1954); Jessup, "Political and Humanitarian Approaches to Limitation of Warfare," 51 Am. J. Int'l L. 757, 759 (1957); Accioly, "Guerre et neutralité en face du droit des gens contemporain" in Mélange Basdevant 1-2, 7 (1960); and Pictet, "The Need to Restore the Laws and Customs Relating to Armed Conflict," Rev. Int'l Comm'n Jur., No. 1 (March 1969), 22, 37.

[14] Actually, the 1907 Hague Regulations (note 9 *supra*) were in large part a comparatively minor revision of the Regulations attached to the 1899 Second Hague Convention, 32 Stat. 1803; 1 Am. J. Int'l L. Supp. 129 (1907).

[15] The following very apt statement appears in Pictet, "The XXth International Conference of the Red Cross: Results in the Legal Field," 7 J. Int'l Comm'n Jur., 3, 11 (1966):

> ". . . whereas the ruined cities [of World War II] have been rebuilt, the States have done nothing to restore the Hague Rules, which vanished under the same ruins . . . While the techniques of offensive action have taken giant strides forward, the only rules which can be invoked date from 1907. Such a situation is flagrant in its absurdity."

The Secretary-General's Report on Respect for Human Rights in Armed Conflict, A/7720, para. 131, is to the same effect, stating that military-technical developments "have brought major changes which the authors of existing international instruments could not envisage." And that many governments share the belief that affirmative action is needed in this area is demonstrated by a number of the answers received by the Secretary-General in response to his inquiry regarding the preparation of A/7720. See the replies of Finland (at 76 of the original United Nations document); Hungary (at 77); Morocco (at 82); Norway (at 82); and Romania (at 85). This Report is, of course, the basis for this paper and for the Fourteenth Hammarskjold Forum of the Association of the Bar of the City of New York. It will be referred to simply as "the Report" or as A/7720, and will be cited as A/7720.

[16] This reluctance on its part, and a similar reluctance on the part of the various subsidiary organs of the United Nations, is noted in A/7720, para. 19.

[17] Resolution XXIII of the International Conference on Human Rights, Teheran, April-May 1968 (United Nations publication, Sales No.: E. 68. XIV 2), at 18.

[18] See Appendix 1 hereto.

[19] See note 15 *supra.*

[20] It will be noted that operative paragraph 1 has now been given a somewhat different emphasis, an emphasis of a type which has tended to permeate all United Nations actions in recent years. It is to be hoped that this will not be to the detriment of a revision and modernization of the general law of war which, of course, is, or should be, largely applicable in both international and internal conflicts.

[21] "Powerful" in the sense that it has strong support from people all over the world who are acquainted with and who welcome its methods and objectives. Apart from its dedication to humanitarian endeavors, the ICRC has found that

> "belligerents necessarily consider this law [of war] as a single whole, and the inadequacy of the rules relating to the conduct of hostilities has a negative impact on the observance of the Geneva Conventions."

ICRC, Reaffirmation 8.

[22] It has been the practice to refer to the rules governing the conduct of hostilities as "Hague" law and to the rules governing the treatment of people (wounded and sick, prisoners of war, civilians) as "Geneva" law. See, for example, Pictet, note 13 *supra,* at 23. There is no merit to such a distinction. The 1899 and the 1907 Hague Regulations dealt with, *inter alia,* prisoners of war and military occupation. Those subjects are now covered in whole or in part by the Third and Fourth 1949 Geneva Conventions, respectively (see note 25 *infra*). And the 1925 Geneva Gas Protocol (see note 84 *infra*) as well as the ICRC's Draft Rules (see note 26 *infra*) are both concerned with permissible weapons, methods of attacks, etc., subjects which are basic to the Hague Regulations. Were it not for the 1954 Hague Cultural Convention (see note 2

supra), it might well be assumed that, the Netherlands no longer having the neutral status which it enjoyed prior to World Warr II, the nations of the world prefer to discuss subjects dealing with hostilities in still-neutral Switzerland. In any event, whether it is "Hague" law governing the conduct of hostilities or "Geneva" law governing the treatment of persons, its ultimate objective is humanitarian in nature.

[23] This new version was the 1929 Geneva Convention for the Amelioration of the Conditions of the Wounded and Sick in Armies in the Field, 47 Stat. 2074; 118 L.N.T.S. 303; 27 Am. J. Int'l L. Supp. 43 (1933).

[24] The 1929 Geneva Convention Relative to the Treatment of Prisoners of War, 47 Stat. 2021; 118 L.N.T.S. 343; 27 Am. J. Int'l L. Supp. 59 (1933).

[25] The 1949 Geneva Convention for the Amelioration of the Conditon of the Wounded and Sick in Armed Forces in the Field (the "First" Convention), 6 U.S.T. 3114; 75 U.N.T.S. 31; the 1949 Geneva Convention for the Amelioration of the Condition of the Wounded, Sick and Shipwrecked Members of Armed Forces at Sea (the "Second" Convention), 6 U.S.T. 3217; 75 U.N.T.S. 85; the 1949 Geneva Convention Relative to the Treatment of Prisoners of War (the "Third" Convention), 6 U.S.T. 3316; 75 U.N.T.S. 135; 47 Am. J. Int'l L. Supp. 119 (1953); and the 1949 Geneva Convention Relative to the Protection of Civilian Persons in Time of War (the "Fourth" Convention), 6 U.S.T. 3516; 75 U.N.T.S. 287; 50 Am. J. Int'l L. Supp. 724 (1956). Regarding this achievement Spaight is reported to have said:

> "The historians of the future will be puzzled by the conclusion of three [*sic*] new Geneva Conventions in 1949, and the failure of the powers who agreed to them to do anything to regulate those methods of war which, if continued, will make the humanitarian provisions of those Conventions read like hypocritical nonsense."

Quoted in Dunbar, "The Legal Regulation of Modern Warfare," 40 Trans. Grot. Soc. 83, 91 (1955).

[26] This is the Fourth Convention, note 25 *supra*. Of course, even the ICRC is not always immediately successful in its humanitarian efforts. In 1957 it presented to the XIXth International Conference of the Red Cross, meeting in New Delhi, its Draft Rules for the Limitation of the Dangers Incurred by the Civilian Population in Time of War. The Conference adopted a resolution requesting the ICRC to transmit the Draft Rules to the Governments. To quote the ICRC Director-General:

> "[T]heir replies took the form of a crushing silence, with the exception of a few well-disposed countries. The great powers, in particular, remained silent . . ."

Pictet, note 15 *supra,* at 12.

[27] Operative subparagraphs 1 (*a*), (*b*), and (*c*) of A/ RES/2444 (XXIII) were taken verbatim from the Red Cross resolution which is itself cited in the opening part of operative paragraph 1 of the United Nations resolution. The General Assembly omitted a fourth paragraph of the Red Cross resolution

which stated "that the general principles of the Law of War apply to nuclear and similar weapons."

[28] See Resolutions X, XI, XII, XIII, XIV, XVII, and XVIII, 9 Int'l Rev. Red Cross 613-19 (1969). Of particular relevance is the following extract from Resolution XIII, in which the Conference

"requests the ICRC on the basis of its report [ICRC, Reaffirmation] to pursue actively its efforts in this regard with a view to:

1. proposing, as soon as possible, concrete rules which would supplement the existing humanitarian law,
2. inviting governmental, Red Cross and other experts representing the principal legal and social systems in the world to meet for consultations with the ICRC on these proposals,
3. submitting such proposals to Governments for their comments, and,
4. if it is deemed advisable, recommending the appropriate authorities to convene one or more diplomatic conferences of States parties to the Geneva Conventions and other interested States, in order to elaborate international legal instruments incorporating those proposals."

[29] As of October 15, 1969, just over 20 years from the date on which they were signed, the four 1949 Geneva Conventions had 125 ratifications and accessions. 9 Int'l Rev. Red Cross 646 (1969). (The data contained in note 49 of A/7720 is incorrect. That contained in Annex IIB of A/7720 is correct.) It should be observed that all of the great powers are Parties to these Conventions. It is interesting to note that the practice of Governments is apparently contrary to the decision of the International Law Commission discussed in the text in connection with note 12 *supra*. Ratifications and accessions to these "war" conventions far exceed those to any of the conventions drafted by the Commission, as important as these latter are.

[30] See text in connection with note 12 *supra*.

[31] ICRC, Reaffirmation 11.

[32] para. 21.

[33] As further evidence of the post-World War II antipathy to the use of the word "war," it might be noted that, apart from Article 107 referring to World War II, it is not used anywhere in the Charter of the United Nations; instead we find such terms as "international disputes," "breaches of peace," "acts of aggression," etc. Universal adoption of the term "armed conflict," a term already familiar to those acquainted with the four 1949 Geneva Conventions and the 1954 Hague Cultural Convention, will certainly result in uniformity of language—even if some who are less able to accept new ideas will, for a time, have to think twice and then say "Oh, you mean the law of war!"

[34] This problem is, of course, also of major importance with respect to internal conflict (civil war) and the question of the application of one of the so-called "common" articles (Article 3) of the 1949 Geneva Conventions.

[35] 36 Stat. 2259; 2 Am. J. Int'l L. Supp. 85 (1908).

36 ". . . Thus the wars of Italy with Abyssinia in 1935, of Japan with China in 1937, of Germany with Poland in 1939, of Russia with Finland in the same year, and of Japan with the United States in 1941, opened without a formal declaration of war."

2 Lauterpacht-Oppenheim, International Law 292-93 (7th ed., 1952). But there were a number of cases of compliance during both World War I (*ibid.*, at 294, footnote 2) and World War II (*ibid.*, at 295, footnote 3).

37 Pictet (ed.), Commentary on the 1949 Geneva Convention Relative to the Treatment of Prisioners of War 19-20 (1960) [hereinafter cited as Pictet, Third Commentary].

38 I Final Record of the Diplomatic Conference of Geneva of 1949, at 47 [hereinafter cited as Final Record]. This is the first paragraph of common Article 2 and is, therefore, identical in Article 2 of each of the four 1949 Geneva Conventions. It is also employed in Article 18 (1) of the 1954 Hague Cultural Convention, *supra* note 2.

39 Pictet, Third Commentary 22-23.

40 Levie, "Maltreatment of Prisoners of War in Vietnam," 48 B.U.L. Rev. 323, 330 (1968); Note, "The Geneva Convention and the Treatment of Prisoners of War in Vietnam," 80 Harv. L. Rev. 851, 858-59 (1967).

41 ICRC, Reaffirmation 94.

42 It is obvious that this proposal jumps squarely into the problem of the enforcement of the law of armed conflict which is, without question, another area requiring major action.

43 IIB Final Record 11 and 16. Further amplification of the proposal, which was clearly required, was not forthcoming and its adoption was not pressed.

44 Annex 21, III Final Record 30.

45 Resolution 2, I Final Record 361. So far as is known, this resolution has never been implemented.

46 In addition, it might be noted that the Security Council undoubtedly already has the power to make such a decision; that it has heretofore, in effect, made such a decision, but always in the context of a call for a cessation of the armed conflict so found to exist (*e.g.*, S/RES/233 (1967), adopted June 6, 1967, in which the Security Council states its concern "at the outbreak of fighting" in the Middle East and calls for "a cessation of all military activities in the area"); and that it has not, and probably will not, ever exercise such power in the context of the proposal under discussion as to do so would be an admission of its inability to eliminate completely the breach of the peace involved.

47 To gain support at the outset and to ensure complete impartiality, it might be denied jurisdiction over fact situations existing at the time of its creation.

48 The General Assembly has, on a number of occasions, called upon its Members "to make effective use of existing facilities for fact-finding" (*e.g.*, A/RES/2330 (XXII)). The present proposal would, in effect, merely create a new specialized fact-finding body and provide for certain results to flow automatically if specified facts are found. It is a variation and expansion of

the Commission of Inquiry originally created by the First Hague Convention of 1899 (32 Stat. 1779; 1 Am. J. Int'l L. Supp. 107 (1907) and applied for the first time in the Dogger Bank Incident (Scott, Hague Court Reports 403 (1916)).

[49] Of course, many additional details of creation and operation would necessarily be included in any convention establishing such a body; but these appear to be unnecessary for the purposes of this paper. However, it should be mentioned that, as in the case of the Protecting Power in the 1949 Geneva Conventions, provision would have to be made for the ICEHRAC to use, when needed, an operational staff.

[50] While it is true that the provision for automatic economic and communications sanctions goes even somewhat beyond the comparable provisions of the Charter of the United Nations, it is suggested that the majority of law-abiding States have come to realize that there will always be a few delinquents among them and that only the absolute knowledge of automatic, effective, and universal sanctions will tend to keep the delinquent States in line. (The sanctions against Rhodesia can scarcely be described with those adjectives!)

[51] Certainly, the 125 ratifications of and accessions to the 1949 Geneva Conventions, which were drafted before many of the acceding States were even in existence as members of the international community, were not obtained merely because of an overwhelming urge on the part of nations to be Parties to it; they were obtained because of moral and humanitarian pressures and because few nations were willing to be pointed at as not having accepted these great humanitarian expressions.

[52] Can there be any great doubt that President Nixon's announcement concerning his intended actions with respect to chemical and biological warfare (see section 3 *infra*) was motivated not only by humanitarian considerations but also by the increasing feeling of isolation which the United States was being compelled to endure in this respect, as well as diplomatic pressure from friends, resolutions of the General Assembly, resolutions of the ICRC, etc.?

[53] Levie, "Prisoners of War and the Protecting Power," 55 Am J. Int'l L. 374, 376 (1961).

[54] *Ibid.,* 377-78.

[55] See note 24 *supra.*

[56] The basic article relating to the Protecting Power is one of the common articles, Article 8/8/8/9. References to this institution appear throughout the Conventions. See Levie, note 53 *supra,* at 380-81, where there is a list of 36 articles in the Prisoner-of-War Convention containing references to the Protecting Power.

[57] Common Article 10/10/10/11 covers this latter subject. The U.S.S.R. and the other Communist countries all reserved to these articles.

[58] A/7720, para. 213.

[59] *Ibid.*

[60] It is probable that the United States has not even attempted to secure the designation of a Protecting Power in Vietnam because such action would appear to constitute a legal recognition not only of North Vietnam as a State, but also, and perhaps more important, of the existence of a state of war.

[61] A/7720, at 78 of the original United Nations document.

[62] *Ibid.*, at 91.

[63] *Ibid.*, para. 215. See also para. 203.

[64] "Nigeria/Biafra: Armed Conflict with a Vengeance," Rev. Int'l Comm'n Jur., No. 2 (June 1969) 10, 13.

[65] See note 28 *supra*. In view of the fact that the 1949 Geneva Conventions clearly indicate that the activities of the Protecting Power and of the ICRC are complementary and not alternative (see Levie, note 53 *supra*, at 394-96), it is difficult to understand why the resolution was phrased in the disjunctive.

[66] ICRC, Reaffirmation, at 7, where the following appears:

". . . This is all the more true in that there is no procedure for supervision which would guarantee the application of these rules [governing the conduct of hostilities]; the impression of inadequacy often also springs from their defective application."

To the same effect see *ibid.*, 87-88.

[67] Common Article 9/9/9/10 is the basic provision of the four 1949 Geneva Conventions relating to the activities of the ICRC. Paragraph 3 of common Article 10/10/10/11, concerning replacements and substitutes for Protecting Powers, permits the ICRC to offer its services to perform the humanitarian functions of the Protecting Power when there is no Protecting Power. This is probably the basis upon which the ICRC has acted in the post-1949 Geneva Conventions era. One of its more successful recent efforts was in connection with the Honduras-Salvador conflict. 9 Int'l Rev. Red Cross 493-96 (1969), no ibid., 95-105 (1970).

[68] A/7720, para. 226. Italy suggested considering the possibility of "delegating authority to the International Red Cross, so that that body may, in the case of armed conflict, ensure that its own representatives are continually present in the belligerent countries throughout the duration of the conflict." *Ibid.*, at 79 of the original United Nations document. A somewhat similar suggestion was made by the group of experts convened by the ICRC. ICRC, Reaffirmation 107.

[69] Le Comité International de la Croix-Rouge et le Conflit de Corée: Recueil des Documents, *passim* (2 vols., 1952); British Ministry of Defence, Treatment of British Prisoners of War in Korea 33-34 (1955).

[70] "The International Committee and the Vietnam Conflict," 6 Int'l Rev. Red Cross 399, 402-03 (1966); St. Louis Post-Dispatch, Feb. 5, 1970, p. 2B, col. 1.

[71] Strangely enough, it has apparently been permitted to function with virtually no restrictions in Israel for the protection of both prisoners of war and of civilians in the occupied territory. See, for example, 8 Int'l Rev. Red Cross 18-19 (1968); 9 *ibid.*, 173-76, 417-19, 488, and 640. On the other hand, the United Nations has encountered some difficulty in making an investigation of the treatment of civilians in the occupied territory because of the Israeli position that the resolution calling for it was biased and one-sided.

However, even the International Conference of the Red Cross found it necessary to express concern about the plight of these people. 9 Int'l Rev. Red Cross 613 (1969).

[72] The Report also makes a suggestion to this latter effect. A/7720, para. 217. It is entirely possible, however, that some States, notably Switzerland and Sweden, which did yeoman work as Protecting Powers during both World Wars, would not wish to shoulder these additional, and potentially controversial, problems. This would make the solution herein suggested all the more necessary. It might be appropriate to cover this eventuality by providing for a possible division of functions, where desired, the Protecting Power, if there be one, performing the traditional functions with respect to wounded and sick, prisoners of war, and civilians, and the substitute performing the function with respect to the conduct of hostilities.

[73] In ICRC, Reaffirmation 89-90, this is ascribed to the fact that many of the conflicts since 1949 have been of an internal nature; but what of Korea, the Yemen, Vietnam, the Middle East, etc.? In none of these conflicts has there been a Protecting Power.

[74] In A/7720, para. 216, it is suggested that a new organ be created which could "offer its services in case the Parties do not exercise their choice." For the reasons already advanced, it is not belived that any system other than one which operates automatically will constitute a solution to the problem.

[75] This calls for selection by one State, acceptance by the State so selected, and approval by the State on whose territory the Protecting Power is to operate. See Levie, note 53 *supra*, at 383.

[76] The Report (A/7720, para. 218) makes two suggestions with respect to the legal effect of the designation of a Protecting Power or of an international organ as a substitute therefor: (1) that the Protecting Power, or the substitute, should be considered as an agent of the international community and not merely of one belligerent State; and (2) that the designation, being solely humanitarian in purpose, should have no legal consequences. The first comment is already true under the 1949 Geneva Conventions, although the term "Parties to the Convention" is deemed appropriate rather than "international community" (see Levie, note 53 *supra*, at 382-83); and the second comment might well be accomplished by the use of a provision such as that appearing in the last paragraph of common Article 3 of the 1949 Conventions: "The application of the preceding provisions shall not affect the legal status of the Parties to the conflict." This provision was eventually applied during the French-Algerian conflict of the late 1950s and early 1960s.

[77] The ICRC experts were also of this opinion. ICRC, Reaffirmation 89 and 91. Had such an international body heretofore existed with such powers and duties, there could have been immediate investigations of allegations of such charges as the use of gas in the Yemen by the United Arab Republic, of bacteriological agents in Korea by the United Nations Command, etc. In this regard, see Joyce, Red Cross International 201 (1959). In fact, it is probably safe to say that under these circumstances many such allegations would never be made in the first place!

[78] The subject is there discussed at length. A/7720, paras. 216-225. Despite the cautious defense of the use of a political organization as a Protecting Power, made in the last paragraph cited, it would appear that, for the

reasons heretofore stated (see text in connection with note 46 *supra*), the creation of a new, non-political body is basically the position taken by the Report.

[79] See note 57 *supra*. The reservations were justified. The article, in effect, authorizes the Detaining Power to unilaterally select a substitute for the Protecting Power. The reservations would merely require agreement on the part of the Power of Origin, as in the case of the selection of the Protecting Power itself. See note 75 *supra*. Of course, were it a Party to the new convention which we are discussing, it would have agreed in advance to the filling of the void by the ICEHRAC.

[80] I Final Record 201. Concerning this resolution, see the text in connection with note 45 *supra*.

[81] Once again, of course, the ICEHRAC would need a fairly large operational staff, including many specialists, to serve as its eyes and ears, to collect and sift evidence. But this is no more than an administrative problem which should present no insurmountable difficulty.

[82] There is no reason whatsoever why, under appropriate legal safeguards (see note 76 *supra*), these provisions could not be made applicable to internal conflicts, and to conflicts of "national liberation," which are frequently much more sanguinary than are international conflicts. "Nigeria/Biafra: Armed Conflict with a Vengeance," *loc. cit.*, note 64 *supra*.

[83] The question will undoubtedly be asked immediately why the present discussion concerning the elimination of chemical and biological weapons does not include nuclear weapons. That matter has been, and continues to be, one of the major subjects of discussion at the meetings of the nuclear powers themselves and at the meetings of the Conference of the Committee on Disarmament (formerly the Eighteen-Nation Committee on Disarmament). The status of these various discussions and the reason for the stalemate which has now existed for more than a decade is well known. It could not conceivably serve any useful purpose for this paper to make a proposal for the banning of nuclear weapons, with or without inspection. Probably only some scientific breakthrough will solve that problem. In the meantime we have what some call "the equilibrium of dissuasion." ICRC, Reaffirmation 50.

[84] The Geneva Protocol for the Prohibition of the Use in War of Asphyxiating, Poisonous or Other Gases and of Bacteriological Methods of Warfare, signed at Geneva on June 17, 1925 (94 L.N.T.S. 65; 25 Am. J. Int'l L. Supp. 94 (1931)), uses the term "bacteriological." Because scientific developments since 1925 have indicated the possible use in armed conflict of various living organisms (*e.g.*, rickettsiae, viruses, and fungi), as well as bacteria, the more inclusive "biological" is now very generally used. In this regard see the Report of the Secretary-General based on the Report of the Group of Consultant Experts, United Nations Document A/7575/Rev. 1, Chemical and Bacteriological (Biological) Weapons and the Effect of Their Possible Use (United Nations publication, Sales No.: E. 69, I. 24), paras. 17-18 [hereinafter cited as UN, CB Weapons]; and Article 1 of the British Draft Convention, note 130 *infra*, which refers to "microbial and other biological agents."

[85] In the Foreword to the Report of the Secretary-General (see UN, CB Weapons, note 84 *supra*, at viii), U Thant quoted as follows from his 1968 Annual Report:

". . . The question of chemical and biological weapons has been overshadowed by the question of nuclear weapons, which have a destructive power several orders of magnitude greater than that of chemical and biological weapons. Nevertheless, these too are weapons of mass destruction regarded with universal horror. In some respects, they may be even more dangerous than nuclear weapons because they do not require the enormous expenditure of financial and scientific resources that are required for nuclear weapons. Almost all countries, including small ones and developing ones, may have access to these weapons, which can be manufactured quite cheaply, quickly and secretly in small laboratories or factories . . ."

[86] A comparatively short list of some of the works in this area will be found in UN, CB Weapons, note 84 *supra,* at 99. To that list should certainly be added McCarthy, The Ultimate Folly: War by Pestilence, Asphyxiation, and Defoliation (1969).

[87] Mention need be made of only two authoritative forums where numerous discussions of this subject have taken place: the United Nations, where it has been discussed at length both in the First Committee and in the General Assembly; and the United States Congress where Representative Richard D. McCarthy and others similarly concerned have not allowed the matter to pass unnoticed. See, for example, N.Y. Times, Nov. 19, 1969, p. 9, col. 1.

[88] One author makes the rather pessimistic evaluation that this recent concern "is perhaps an index of the growing role of such weapons in military preparations." Brownlie, "Legal Aspects of CBW" in Rose (ed.), CBW: Chemical and Biological Warfare 141, 150-51 (1968). [This collection hereinafter cited as Rose, CBW].

[89] For a short but comprehensive history of the use or alleged use of chemicals in warfare, from the Peloponnesian Wars to Korea, see Kelly, "Gas Warfare in International Law," 9 Mil. L. Rev. 3-14 and *passim* (1960).

[90] Declaration of St. Petersburg of 1868 Renouncing the Use, in Time of War, of Explosive Projectiles, 1 Am. J. Int'l L. Supp. 95 (1907).

[91] See note 14 *supra.*

[92] 1 Am. J. Int'l L. Supp. 157 (1907). The United States did not sign or ratify this Declaration.

[93] See note 9 *supra.*

[94] Article 171, Treaty of Versailles, 3 Malloy (Redmond), Treaties, 3331, 3402; 13 Am. J. Int'l L. Supp. 151, 230 (1919). While the United States did not ratify this Treaty, it did ratify the Treaty of Berlin (42 Stat. 1939; 16 Am. J. Int'l L. Supp. 10 (1922)), which incorporates by reference Article 171 of the Treaty of Versailles.

[95] 3 Malloy (Redmond) Treaties 3116; 16 Am J. Int'l L. Supp. 57 (1922).

[96] A/7720, para. 53.

[97] See note 84 *supra.*

[98] A/7720, note 31 and Annex II, Tables I and II.

[99] This latter reservation preserves the right to use chemical and bacteriological agents as a reprisal for their first use by the enemy. Some

writers would not even permit this use; and there is no doubt that an alleged reprisal can be the excuse for a first strike.

[100] Spaight, Air Power and War Rights 192-93 (3d ed., 1947).

[101] Meselson, "Ethical Problems: Preventing CBW," in Rose, CBW 163.

[102] As the former Assistant Secretary of Defense, Carter Burgess, later said:

> "It has been reported that following the Korean conflict there were no flies in China. Allegedly, the 'germ warfare' propaganda of the Red Chinese was so effective that it incited a universal attack on these insects by the Chinese people."

"Foreword: Prisoners of War," 56 Col. L. Rev. 676 (1956).

[103] Viney, "Research Policy: Soviet Union," in Rose, CBW 130,133.

[104] Meselson, "CBW in Use: The Yemen," in Rose, CBW 99 and 101.

[105] See note 26 *supra.*

[106] See, for example, A/RES/2162B (XXI), 5 December 1966; A/RES/2454A (XXIII), 20 December 1968; and A/RES/2603B (XXIV), 16 December 1969.

[107] A/RES/2603A (XXIV), 16 December 1969.

[108] See, for example, Brownlie, note 88 *supra,* at 143-44; and O'Brien, "Biological/Chemical Warfare and the International Law of War," 51 Geo. L.J. 1, 36 (1962).

[109] There are 68 Parties to the 1925 Geneva Protocol after 45 years, compared to 125 Parties to the 1949 Geneva Conventions after 20 years.

[110] U.S. Army Field Manual 27-10, The Law of Land Warfare, para. 38 (1956). While there is no explicit denial of the existence of a customary prohibition, this appears inherent in the tenor of the phraseology used. For an elaboration of the United States position, see 10 Whiteman, Digest of International Law, 455-56 (1968).

[111] See note 52 *supra.*

[112] N.Y. Times, Nov. 26, 1969, p. 16, col. 1; 61 Dept. State Bull. 541 (1969).

[113] On February 14, 1970, President Nixon ordered the destruction of all toxins which had been produced for weapons purposes. St. Louis Post-Dispatch, Feb. 15, 1970, p. 1, col. 1. These apparently had been overlooked in the original announcement.

[114] It would almost seem as though, after years of exploiting the fact that the United States had not ratified the Protocol, the Soviet Union is now determined to place roadblocks in the announced intention of the United States to accept a prohibition on the use of biological weapons. In addition to its usual adamant objection to any treaty calling for verification procedures, it is now apparently insisting on a new agreement which would replace the 1925 Protocol and simultaneously ban both chemical and biological weapons, rather than retaining the old agreement and supplementing it with a new treaty prohibiting biological weapons as proposed by the British and accepted by the United States. St. Louis Post-Dispatch, Feb. 17, 1970, p. 2A, col. 1.

This latter dispute appears to be one of procedure, rather than substance, and the Soviet approach might well afford the opportunity for the necessary clarifications discussed immediately below.

[115] ICRC, Reaffirmation 58. See also A/7720, para. 201.

[116] N.Y. Times, Feb. 3, 1970, p. 3, col. 6.

[117] UN, CB Weapons, para. 20.

[118] Meselson, "Ethical Problems: Preventing CBW," in Rose, CBW 163, 167.

[119] *Ibid.* See also UN, CB Weapons, para. 374.

[120] Sidel, "Napalm," in Rose, CBW 44, 46.

[121] Ramundo, Peaceful Coexistence 138-39 (1967). It was recently reported that a suit had been filed against the Dow Chemical Co., formerly the chief manufacturer of napalm for the United States armed forces, alleging that Dow had supplied the United States with "various types of chemical, biological, bacteriological, incendiary and asphyxiatory weapons" and asking that it be designated a "war criminal." St. Louis Post-Dispatch, Feb. 3, 1970, p. 2A, col. 4. There is a certain resemblance to *The Zyklon B Case,* 1 L. Rep. Tr. War Crim. 93.

[122] ICRC, Reaffirmation 61-62; A/7720, paras. 198-99.

[123] ICRC, Reaffirmation 62-63; Brownlie, note 88 *supra,* at 150. The U.S. Army Field Manual 27-10, The Law of Land Warfare (1956) states (at para. 18) that while its use is not violative of international law, it should not be employed in such a way as to cause unnecessary suffering.

[124] A/7720, para. 200. See also Sidel, note 120 *supra.*

[125] Galston, "Defoliants," in Rose, CBW 62; UN, CB Weapons, para. 311. The scientific problem is not far removed from the current problem in the United States arising out of the use of DDT and other pesticides.

[126] Nor has it been satisfactorily established that defoliants will not in time adversely affect human health.

[127] ". . . The tremendous capabilities of modern weapons of mass destruction, however, make the objective of their effectively sanctioned abolition much more urgent than was weapons abolition at the time of the Hague Conference."

Mallison, "The Laws of War and the Juridical Control of Weapons of Mass Destruction in General and Limited Wars," 36 Geo. Wash. L. Rev. 308, 321 (1967).

[128] UN, CB Weapons, para. 375; ICRC, Reaffirmation 57; Meselson, note 101 *supra,* at 169. See also the U Thant statement, note 85 *supra;* and Mallison, note 127 *supra,* at 324.

[129] Malek, "Biological Weapons," in Rose, CBW 48, 56; Humphrey, "Ethical Problems: Preventing CBW," *ibid.,* at 157, 159. The Stockholm International Peace Research Institute is currently engaged in a project to determine "whether it is technically possible to discover production of biological agents on a scale of military relevance."

[130] Revised Draft Convention for the Prohibition of Biological Methods of Warfare," A/7720, at 87 of the original United Nations document; N.Y. Times, Nov. 26, 1969, p. 16, col. 5.

[131] Memorandum presented to the British War Cabinet on August 17, 1917. Quoted in "Air Power," 1 Enc. Brit. 449, 450 (1970).

[132] The possible use of nuclear weapons, whether delivered by ballistic missiles or by bombers, merely emphasizes the gravity of the problem under discussion.

[133] Lauterpacht, note 13 *supra,* at 365-66.

[134] See note 4 *supra.*

[135] Regulations attached to the Fourth Hague Convention of 1907, note 9 *supra.*

[136] Stone, note 1 *supra,* 621, footnote 91.

[137] Ninth Hague Convention of 1907 Concerning Bombardment by Naval Forces in Time of War, 36 Stat. 2351; 2 Am. J. Int'l L. Supp. 146 (1908).

[138] Tracer bullets were used, apparently without objection from either side, despite the 1868 Declaration of St. Petersburg (note 90 *supra*) which outlawed explosive and incendiary projectiles. Apparently it is generally accepted that this prohibition does not apply to aircraft. See Article 18 of the Hague Air Rules, note 140 *infra.*

[139] Spaight, note 100 *supra,* at 41-42 and 244-50. The disillusioned will say that successful weapons are never outlawed and seldom restricted in their use.

[140] 17 Am. J. Int'l L. Supp. 245 (1923); 32 Am. J. Int'l L. Supp. 12 (1938); Greenspan, The Modern Law of Land Warfare 650 (1959). These Rules were drafted by an eminent Commission of Jurists convened by resolution of the Conference at which the Treaty of Washington, note 95 *supra,* was drafted.

[141] Quoted in Spaight, note 100 *supra,* at 257. These limitations on air bombardment were included in a resolution adopted by the Assembly of the League of Nations on September 28, 1938. *Ibid.,* at 258.

[142] Actually, the Germans had already bombed Warsaw, obliterating much of it.

[143] Pictet, note 13 *supra,* at 30. After the Germans had disregarded the principles of the military objective and of the protection of the civilian population in Norway, the Netherlands, and Belgium in April-May 1940, the British announced that they reserved to themselves "the right to take any action which they consider appropriate in the event of the bombing by the enemy of civilian populations." Spaight, note 100 *supra,* at 264-266.

[144] Pictet, note 13 *supra,* at 30.

[145] Lauterpacht, note 13 *supra,* at 366, footnote 1. Of course, in a somewhat parallel situation, where both sides had followed substantially the same course of conduct, unrestricted submarine warfare, the International Military Tribunal refused to assess any punishment on this score against German Admiral Doentiz.

[146] Spaight, note 100 *supra,* at 277. And he does not stand alone. Pictet, note 13 *supra,* at 39.

[147] The former use of the term "undefended" as a basis for determining that an area is not subject to attack appears to have lost significance—and properly so.

[148] Lauterpacht, note 13 *supra,* at 364.

[149] A/7720, para. 131.

[150] ICRC, Reaffirmation 39; Spaight, note 100 *supra,* at 43-44 and 47.

[151] Lauterpacht, note 13 *supra,* at 369. See also Pictet, note 13 *supra,* at 38; and "Nigeria/Biafra: Armed Conflict with a Vengeance," note 64 *supra,* at 10-11. The Report, A/7720, para. 144, points out that terror bombing "is more frequently than not counterproductive."

[152] See Spaight, note 100 *supra,* at 43.

[153] A/7720, para. 140-141. Of course, for propaganda purposes, even if every bomb dropped by an attacking airplane landed in the middle of a tank park, the enemy will mention only the deaths of a woman and her two children—who had had the misfortune to pick that time to hawk bottled pop to the tank crews.

[154] Spaight, note 100 *supra,* at 47. Other apt quotations from this authoritative, but frequently controversial, work are (at 43):

> "The position was that, for the first time, belligerents had at their disposal an instrument enabling them to strike not only at the *user* of armaments but at the *makers* of armaments. The possession of such an instrument had the effect of calling in question the hitherto accepted distinction between armed forces and civilians, between combatants and noncombatants. . . .
>
> "It was a praiseworthy principle in the circumstances of the pre-air age of war, but it was not one which could survive the arrival of the bombing aircraft. For, objectively considered, it was not a logical principle. . . ."

[155] *Ibid.* 254, 270, 271.

[156] Meyrowitz, "Reflections on the Centenary of the Declaration of St. Petersburg," 8 Int'l Rev. Red Cross 611, 620-21 (1968).

[157] A/7720, para. 143.

[158] Unfortunately, as stated by one author, "(i)t is far easier to moralize about air attacks on civilians, and to offer soothing verbal solutions, and to dismiss target area bombing as probably unlawful, than to frame rules for mitigation of human suffering with some hope of belligerent observance amid the realities of war." Stone, note 1 *supra,* at 627.

[159] A/7720, paras. 145-150.

[160] Note 25 *supra.*

[161] Note 26 *supra.*

[162] ICRC, Reaffirmation 73.

[163] Based on Article 6 of the ICRC Draft Rules and Article 22 of the Hague Air Rules.

[164] Based on Article 10 of the ICRC Draft Rules.

[165] Based on one of the ICRC principles.

[166] Based on one of the ICRC principles.

[167] Based on Article 7 of the ICRC Draft Rules and on a proposal of the Institut de Droit International.

PART TWO

THE FORUM PROCEEDINGS

Introductory Remarks of John Carey, Chairman Special Committee on the Lawyer's role in the Search for Peace, The Association of the Bar of the City of New York.

It is a pleasure to welcome all of you to the Fourteenth Hammerskjold Forum presented by the Special Committee on the Lawyers Role in the Search for Peace. For those of you who may be unfamiliar with this program, the Committee was established in 1961 to stimulate discussion among lawyers with respect to the problems of peace, and more particularly, to examine the ways in which law can contribute to peaceful settlement of the issues that divide men and nations.

The Committee has sponsored over the years a series of programs in which eminent scholars, lawyers, and diplomats have graciously contributed their talents and time to the discussion of some of the burning international problems of our time. In most cases, the programs presented at the Bar Association have been supplemented, or perhaps more accurately, completed by publication in a small volume of the special background papers prepared for the programs and summaries of the proceedings of each Forum. The Library of the Bar Association has very kindly provided excellent bibliographies for the books. The most recent volume contains the background paper and proceedings of the Thirteenth Hammerskjold Forum which focussed on Prospects for Peace in the Middle East.

Tonight we turn our attention to an extremely important and topical subject: the way in which legal protection can be afforded to individuals caught in the throes of battle. The title chosen— "When Battle Rages, How Can Law Protect?"—is deliberately vague so that our speakers can bring the full extent of their experience and knowledge to bear on the many issues encompassed and suggested by the title.

In his excellent working paper, prepared especially for tonight's forum, Professor Howard Levie draws our attention to the fact that comparatively little attention has been paid during our century to the development and improvement of international law with respect to the rules of war and the protection of civilians and non-combatants. He explains this by pointing to the hopes of the world that after two devastating world conflagrations, war had, in effect, been outlawed by the Treaty of Versailles and the Charter of the United Nations. In addition, it was felt that public opinion might interpret the study of new rules of war and measures to protect civilians and non-combatants in time of war as showing a lack of confidence in the ability of post-war institutions to maintain peace.

Unfortunately, as the years have progressed, we have been forced to accept the fact that war in many different forms continues to be an every day reality. In many different parts of the world persons find themselves involved in or at the mercy of the rigors and effects of armed conflict. The great majority of these persons are not there by choice. They are often civilians whose homes happen to be located in a combat zone. Even combatants today are in large part involved as conscripts rather than as volunteers fighting for a cause. For many participants in the conflict there is the difficult post-combat status of prisoner of war, perhaps wounded. It is to the plight of all these individuals that tonight's forum addresses itself. There is little disagreement with the proposition that the organized international community *must* find *some* way to provide as much protection for such individuals as can be afforded in time of armed conflict.

If there can be any doubt about the relevancy of this subject, it is sad to recall that today, March 16, is the second anniversary of the alleged massacres at My Lai, about which we have heard so much through the news media in the last few months and for which several American military men will be placed on trial in the near future. It is also just over two years that the bodies of many victims of reprisals were discovered at Hue following the occupation of that city by the forces of the National Liberation Front or Viet Cong during the Tet offensive in Viet Nam. Another subject currently in the news which is related to tonight's topic is the situation of American prisoners of war in North Vietnam, about which there is disagreement over the applicability of the existing rules concerning the treatment of prisoners of war and the information which should be provided about such prisoners. Nor does the relevance of tonight's subject stem only from the war in Vietnam. During the last few years our newspapers have contained too many stories about the plight of civilians and individuals in many different parts of the world during various forms of armed strife.

Recently the attention of the world as represented at the United Nations has turned to this subject. In May, 1968, the U.N.'s International Conference of Human Rights held in Teheran adopted a resolution which requested the General Assembly to invite the Secretary General of the United Nations to study the need for

> additional humanitarian international conventions or for possible revision of existing Conventions to ensure the better protection of civilians, prisoners and combatants in all armed conflicts and the prohibition and limitation of the use of certain methods and means of warfare.

This resolution led to the adoption of further resolutions by the General Assembly urging study of the above matters and to the preparation of a report by the Secretary General entitled "Respect for Human Rights in Armed Conflict." This report, U.N. Document A/7720, was submitted to the Third Committee of the General Assembly in November, 1969, and is presently being studied by the members of that Committee. At the same time the U.N. has been experimenting with a new way of implementing the Geneva Conventions, through investigation by a small group established by the Commission on Human Rights. The area of investigation is the Israeli-occupied Arab territories.

New issues have arisen due to the international effects of what used to be regarded as strictly internal conflicts. New kinds of weapons, new technologies, new ways of waging war, and concurrently new ways of causing suffering to civilians and combatants underline the need for study of the inadequacies of the existing law and proposals for new law. Our forum tonight will examine some of these issues and hopefully include some recommendations which can contribute to the search for effective solutions to the problem.

Introduction of Mr. Marc Schreiber

Our first speaker this evening is Mr. Marc Schreiber. Mr. Schreiber is an example of a rare type of lawyer who actually practices public international law. A Belgian citizen, he began his career as an attorney in Brussels and as an Assistant Professor at the University of Brussels. During World War II Mr. Schreiber served with the Belgian Government in Exile as an Assistant to Foreign Minister Paul Henri Spaak and as an Associate Legal Advisor. He joined the United Nations at its inception, attending the San Francisco Conference in 1945, and served for many years with distinction as Senior Legal Officer and then as Deputy Director of the Legal Division of the Secretariat. Mr. Schreiber attended numerous conferences and participated in several field missions as legal advisor and as representative of the Secretary-General. The author of a book on the history of Belgium, written at a time when the citizens of that country were under foreign occupation, Mr. Schreiber has also written several articles on developments in the field of international law in which the United Nations has played a role.

In 1966, Mr. Schreiber was named Director of the U.N. Human Rights Division by Secretary General U Thant. During his tenure, the covenants on Human Rights have been adopted by the U.N. General Assembly, the Convention on Racial Discrimination has come into effect, and the Declaration on Discrimination Against Women was adopted. In addition, Mr. Schreiber's office has held seminars in various parts of the world to discuss specific aspects of human rights problems. More recently, he presented to the Third Committee of the General Assembly the Secretary General's Report on Respect for Human Rights in Armed Conflicts. A/7720. It is with great pleasure that I now turn the microphone over to Mr. Marc Schreiber.

Statement of Mr. Schreiber

I thank you very much Mr. Carey. It is indeed a pleasure for me to be here among fellow lawyers. My task of introducing the problem to you is of course made much easier by the excellent paper which Professor Levie has presented and which describes the question briefly and very much to the point. But perhaps I may first try to speak to those of you who have certain inclinations to superstition or who according to the present vogue indulge in astrology.

Among the basic texts which we are going to discuss today are the Hague Regulations on the conduct of warfare, which were adopted around 1907 and which because of the slowness of communication really became known and operative in 1909. The second important instrument is the one which was adopted in Geneva in 1929 and which clarified in an excellent manner the rules of humanitarian law, the international law relating to prisoners of war, and the sick and the wounded on the battlefield. Now the third set of instruments, the four Geneva Conventions which are really the core of our subject, were adopted in 1949.

Our own movement, after the International Conference on Human Rights in Teheran in 1968, really got moving on the problem of human rights in armed conflicts in 1969, so there must be some kind of mysterious force or interplay between stars and planets which incites international lawyers and the international community to make every twenty years an important move in the direction of bringing a little bit more humanity in something mankind tries to prevent with more or less success, i.e. war and armed conflict.

The subject is important. I do not have to stress it. Perhaps a certain degree of optimism may be deserved if we try to remember the attitudes of people let us say twenty years ago and think of the present day's conflicts like the one what recently ended in Nigeria, or the ones still continuing in Vietnam or in the Middle East. There is one point which no one would seriously contest, i.e. that the degree of international concern for the persons affected, the victims of these armed conflicts, the interest in and sensitiveness to their problems have increased very considerably in recent years. Information media which make us aware by sight and sound of the suffering involved have of course greatly contributed to this process. For instance it may be said that only twenty years ago to those of us from Western Europe or the United States the Nigerian internal conflict would have appeared as another war between African tribes; today it has provoked deep emotional outbursts and a sense of personal involvement the world over. We are not going to dwell on that much further.

The problem is also interesting and challenging for lawyers. Here we have texts which have been carefully prepared and which have been ratified by a great number of states and which are not being applied or only partially applied in the form or spirit in which they were written. We have international law which does not keep pace with the technology, with developments in methods of modern warfare. Finally, as I will point out a little later, we encounter a number of traditional legal concepts and definitions which appear to be more in the nature of obstacles than sources for humanitarian solutions.

But the first question to be answered may be the following: why does the U.N. now pay attention to this problem whicle it did not do so for such a long time? Or you may put the question alternatively as: why did the U.N. not pay attention to this particular problem for such a long time?

53

The reason very briefly is a simple one. The U.N. was established to prevent international wars and not to regulate the manner in which wars would be conducted. It must be admitted after all that the U.N. has been pretty successful in stopping international wars, even if it has not been wholly successful in finding permanent solutions. And then the U.N. was prohibited by Article 2 (7) of the Charter from interfering in matters which are essentially within the domestic jurisdiction of states, and what appears at first sight to be more essentially within such domestic jurisdiction than a civil war? The field was one in which the International Red Cross had been active, and maybe that was another reason why the U.N. did not until recently tackle the problem.

Now how did the U.N. involvement begin? It did not begin as an attempt to promote, codify or improve international law. It happened because of the humanitarian element, because of the strength of the emotions in response to sufferings generated by prevailing conflicts at the time of the International Conference on Human Rights which met in Teheran in 1968 during the International Year for Human Rights. The conference adopted the resolution to which Mr. Carey referred, the resolution which states first of all that peace is the underlying condition for the full observance of human rights and war is their negation, that the violence and brutality of our times including massacres, summary executions, tortures and inhuman treatment of prisoners, killing of civilians in armed conflicts and the use of chemical and biological means of warfare including napalm bombing erode human rights and engender counterbrutality. Then the resolution expresses the conviction that even during periods of armed conflicts humanitarian principles must prevail. Hence the request to the General Assembly to ask the Secretary General to study how existing international conventions can be better applied and how they can be improved by appropriate revisions or additions.

Now the General Assembly did not simply make that request to the Secretary General to prepare a study. It adopted at the same time three principles which the International Red Cross and Red Cross Conferences had previously put forward but which had not received much response from governments: (1) that the right of the parties to a conflict to adopt means of injuring the enemy is not unlimited, (2) that it is prohibited to launch attacks against the civilian population as such, and (3) that distinction must be made at all times between persons taking part in the hostilities and members of the civilian population to the effect that the latter should be spared as much as possible.

All that is very general. It is also basic and important. Since the adoption by the General Assembly of these principles, they seem to have been more rapidly accepted as part of accepted principles of international law, and the International Committee of the Red Cross seems very satisfied by this confirmation of the principles by all members of the U.N. Thus we undertook the study hand in hand with the International Committee of the Red Cross.

Now in the United Nations, when the Secretary General or the Secretariat undertakes studies like that, they are not theoretical studies nor enunciations of general principles or of ideal but unreachable solutions. What we do is to try to analyse as exactly as possible what is the situation which we want to remedy, what is the existing law, what has been the United Nations approach to problems touched upon and what can realistically be achieved, taking into account the positions of the major powers, groups of smaller powers and other current preoccupations and then try to foresee what are, in fact, the difficulties which we encounter. In a field where there were recent histories of conflicts and various sensibilities of governments, of course, we had to think twice. So we examined the field of existing international law. The Hague Regulations of 1907 concerning conduct during combat possess an incontestible value and strength, because the Nuremberg Tribunal found them to be declaratory of laws and customs of war. But they employ language rather difficult to apply today, because of the time at which these Regulations were adopted; their authors were ignorant of our present methods of war.

Then there is the 1925 Geneva Protocol on the "ABC" armaments, the asphixiating arms, the bacteriological weapons, and the chemical weapons, again adopted somewhat accidentally during a Disarmament Conference, prohibiting the use of these weapons by those who ratify, but probably still requiring elaboration and measures of implementation. Finally, the four Geneva Conventions on sick and wounded, on land and on sea, on prisoners and on civilian populations.

We were struck by one fact. There are one hundred twenty-five parties to these Geneva Conventions. The Swiss Federal Council, the depository of instruments of ratification, was very liberal. It accepted ratifications from wherever they came, and these are probably international instruments that have been ratified by

55

more countries than any other convention. Thus they constitute a very solid and widely accepted body of international law. The conclusion is obvious: one should not touch such a body of international law unless one has something better to replace it with and unless one is certain that the replacement will be similarly endorsed by the international community.

We examined the provisions of the Geneva conventions and found a great number of excellent principles, a very complete system of law as regards prisoners of war, the sick and wounded, and also with regard to populations of territories occupied as a result of armed conflict. These things were written under the impact of the suffering of these various categories of people during the second World War.

The problem became apparent that these texts have not been or are not fully applied in present day conflicts or not invoked at all. It makes a very big difference whether they are applied or not. Those of us who remember the second World War know very well what a difference it could make to be recognized as prisoners of war, to have that status or not to have it; that could make the difference between life and death or between an uncomfortable but tolerable passage of years in a prisoner camp and complete moral and physical degradation.

The problem is then that the texts exist but are not fully applied; the next inquiry is why, and the question in our mind was, are these texts sufficiently known? There are over four hundred provisions in the four Geneva Conventions. Are these provisions sufficiently known by those who have to apply them, those who actually are in combat or in charge of the occupation of enemy territory and who have sometimes, during the excitment and passion of combat, to exercise rapid judgment and make rapid decisions? There is a problem of education in the so-called humanitarian law. How much are these provisions taught at military schools or universities? How much indoctrination do the armed forces receive in them? I cannot dwell on that; I just leave the problem with you.

The second difficulty is that the conduct of warfare has changed. The existing rules do not even refer to war by weapons of mass destruction. How to protect human rights should these arms be used is beyond anybody's possibility of judgment or evaluation. But the modern trends of warfare, air warfare, submarine warfare, and blitzkrieg, all that does not seem to have sufficiently penetrated the existing texts. We still have the impression by studying them that it is the 19th century, the early 20th century type of warfare which is being dealt with; the declaration of war and the ambassadors who go back to their countries and armies which settle into fronts that hardly move for a long period of time, for many years. All that has changed. There are concepts of the international law of war which are the basis of the existing instruments; references to belligerence in international conflicts as distinguished from conflicts of an internal nature; the distinction between combatants, whom you may destroy in any way you may be able to, and civilians, whom you should not touch but should protect. One concludes that these legal concepts in the conventions do not facilitate your humanitarian task because "wars" are not declared any more. They have not been very often declared since the adoption of the Geneva Conventions.

Because the so-called internal conflicts have so many elements of foreign intervention and because the two parties to a conflict do not necessarily agree that the conflict is international or that it is internal, civilians, when they are in the war zone, escape with great difficulty from the impact of modern weapons. The combatants themselves may perhaps deserve consideration. This rigidity of definitions and these distinctions, while understandable to a lawyer, are easy to invoke in order to pretend that the Conventions are not applicable. But if they are not applicable, then you are entirely at the mercy of whatever humanitarian attitudes parties to the conflict may have. Therefore a legal approach is not necessarily the most fruitful one in the problem which we have to examine.

The human rights approach, the humanitarian approach, the compassionate approach on the contrary leads to certain results. First we notice that in fact the basic United Nations instruments on human rights, whether it is the Charter or whether it is the Universal Declaration on Human Rights, the Convention on Genocide, that on Racial Discrimination, the United Nations Covenants on Human Rights have not made a distinction when they proposed to states obligations with respect to the protection of human rights. They do not distinguish periods of peace from periods of armed conflict. U.N. standards are specifically applicable at all times and everywhere. There are possibilities of derogation, but there are certain human rights from which under the United Nations Covenant on Civil and Political Rights you cannot derogate even in time of war. The Convention on Genocide states specifically that it is applicable both in war time and in peace time. If you take this humanitarian, compassionate approach, it does not matter very much whether the conflict is defined as an international one or a conflict of an internal character.

Finally, the combatant, the soldier himself, must be also protected against abuse. Not every method of annihilation invented by scientists should be permissible to destroy him. Greater attention is now being attracted to that part of the problem. This week the American Veteran's Committee is holding a series of meetings in Washington on the right of combatants during a war. I was very glad to hear that the Department of Defense and the State Department are sending distinguished speakers to address that conference. I was very happy myself to accept an invitation to go there.

There are certain provisions of the Geneva Conventions which seem to be good provisions, but some of them have never been applied in the many armed conflicts since 1949. There are two of them in particular: the provision which provides for the possibility of establishing sanctuaries, safety zones I think they are called in the Convention. They are parts of the territory of parties to an armed conflict where women, children, wounded, sick persons can find refuge. It would be understood that those zones, those sanctuaries, would not be involved in any phase of the conflict, and would therefore be respected. In the report of the Secretary-General to the General Assembly, we have tried to pursue this concept. Would it not be possible to find conditions under which such sanctuaries, for persons who are in no way involved in the war effort, would be admitted, provided there is no participation whatsoever of those areas in the war effort? Would it not be possible to devise such a system, even in time of peace, and make provisions for inspection which would guarantee that the sanctuaries would be set aside only for those who cannot influence the issue of the conflict one way or the other?

Professor Levie does not find this idea particularly promising, but there is another idea on which Professor Levie goes even a little further than we do in the U.N. study. That is another part of the Geneva Conventions which has not been applied. More and more the international community becomes aware of the fact that it is not enough to impose obligations on states and rely on the States which are responsible for fulfilling these obligations. It is necessary to observe the implementation of these obligations by the States, using methods devised by the international community. The supervision of the application of the Geneva Conventions is based on a system of Protecting Powers, and on the somewhat limited role of the International Committee of the Red Cross. This means that by agreement the belligerents accept that certain countries, usually neutral countries, would on their behalf see to it that the other parties respect the requirements of humanitarian law.

That system worked satisfactorily during the First World War. It worked more or less satisfactorily during the Second World War, where Switzerland and Sweden served as protecting powers on both sides. But the system of protecting powers has not received any real application in the conflicts which have arisen since the Geneva Conventions of 1949 were adopted. The system provides that when there are no protecting powers, international organizations, public or private, provided they are independent and objective, could perform that role. That has not worked either. There is a role for the Red Cross; usually the International Committee of the Red Cross proposes its services. Sometimes the services are accepted; sometimes they are not accepted. On the whole, the International Committee of the Red Cross has to work under very difficult conditions.

This is an aspect of the conventions which does not work. We would like to study how to bring about a workable system. Professor Levie envisages the possibility of a special international organization, impartial and objective, which could perform that task. He also refers rightly to the problem of the bombing of cities, air warfare in its various aspects. There is another problem which we mentioned and to which attention could be paid: the fact that all the international effort to provide foodstuffs or medical supplies, all forms of aid to the victims of international conflict, has in fact no basis, or very little basis, on international law. All these efforts depend on the good will of those who give and the good will and the conditions imposed by those who receive.

Those are some of the problems which we will try to study further. As I said, the United Nations Secretary-General cooperates very closely with the International Committee of the Red Cross. The International Committee, I think, finds advantages in having political support and acceptance by the members of the United Nations. We find the experience, the good will and the

59

activities of the International Committee of the Red Cross indispensible.

So I submit for your review and comments the study which was initiated in U.N. Document A/7720. It has been well received by the General Assembly and the Commission on Human Rights, is being studied now by many governments, and will be discussed again at the next session of the General Assembly. We will continue that study and we will seek the advice and cooperation of the best available experts in the field. But we are very happy that more and more private groups, universities, institutions and bar associations, are devoting time to this problem. It is a challenging problem. It is not only an intellectual exercise or even a legal challenge; it is a matter of applying our moral concepts to some of the most dramatic realities of today.

I would like to end by saying that I think it is very proper and appropriate that a Hammarskjold Forum should be devoted to this problem. Mr. Hammarskjold left a mark which is a durable one, if not a permanent one, on all of us who serve the international community. This is the kind of problem which I would say is a problem of his size. This is a kind of intractable problem in many aspects, to which he would have wanted to devote his efforts and his attention.

Introduction of Professor Howard S. Levie

Our next speaker is Professor Howard Levie of St. Louis University Law School. Professor Levie is a graduate of Cornell University and its Law School. He practised law in New York for 12 years before entering the U. S. Army in 1942, where he served until 1963. He retired as a Colonel in the Judge Advocate General's Corps. During his Army service, Professor Levie spent one year at the Korean Armistice Negotiations at Pan Mun Jom. He also served as legal advisor to the U. S. European Command in Paris and occupied the post of Chief of the International Affairs Division of the Judge Advocate General's Office. Since retiring from the Army, Professor Levie has taught at St. Louis University Law School, where he became a full professor in 1965. He has drawn on his experience to write several articles about the treatment of prisoners of war. He brings to tonight's subject his understanding of the problems from a military point of view, as well as his scholarly analysis of the existing rules of international law. We are extremely grateful to Professor Levie for his clear and well-written Working Paper on some major inadequacies of the existing law relating to the protection of individuals during armed conflict.

Statement of Professor Levie

As Mr. Carey pointed out, the Working Paper is entitled *"Some Major Inadequacies* etc." I want to emphasize that, because it does not purport to be all-inclusive, and I do not contend that my subjects of discussion would necessarily be your subjects of discussion–although I am sure that there would be considerable overlap. I know that there are many other important areas which could be discussed; but time and space factors made it necessary that I make a selection, and that selection is entirely my own and not necessarily that of anyone else.

Let me start by pointing out to you that the law of war (that's a nasty word now, we don't say "war" anymore, we say "armed conflict"), the law of armed conflict falls into two categories. We have developed the custom of denominating these two categories as "Hague" law and "Geneva" law, Hague law being the law that governs the conduct of hostilities and Geneva law being the so-called humanitarian law, the law dealing with the protection of persons. I say "so-called" because in my opinion the law of armed conflict, or the law of war, is all humanitarian law. It does not make much difference whether the law says that you cannot use a particular weapon because it causes unnecessary suffering, or whether you say that this particular person is now out of combat because he is a prisoner of war, or that he was never in combat because he is a civilian, and therefore you must give him certain specified treatment. There is not much basic difference between those two types of provisions. They are both humanitarian provisions. Therefore, in my opinion, the entire field of the law of armed conflict with which we are dealing tonight is humanitarian law.

Mr. Schreiber pointed out to you that very little work has been done in the so-called Hague area since 1907 (or since 1909 for the purpose of the twenty-year jumps). As a matter of fact, the 1907 law for the most part dates back to 1899 and probably came into being because of events which had occurred during the Franco-Prussian War of 1870. So Hague law really dates back 100 years and we have very little law governing the conduct of hostilities which has been enacted, if we can use that term with respect to international law, during the past century, apart from the Geneva Gas Protocol of 1925.

On the other hand, in the so-called Geneva area, we find that there has been considerable activity. In 1906 the old Geneva Convention, the so-called Red Cross Convention on sick and wounded, was redrafted. In 1929 not only was it redrafted again, but for the first time a Convention was drafted dealing exclusively with the problem of prisoners of war. (Previously, this subject had been dealt with in a chapter of the 1907 Hague Regulations.) In 1949 not only were these two Conventions redrafted, but for the first time a Convention was drafted dealing exclusively with the problem of civilians.

I attribute all of that activity in the Geneva area to the efforts of the ICRC, the International Committee of the Red Cross. They were interested in the humanitarian field, dealing with people, and their interest was such that they were able to get action. As Mr. Schreiber pointed out, the number of ratifications and accessions to the Geneva Conventions of 1949 (over 125) indicates that if you give the nations something specific to consider you will get ratifications and accessions. Unfortunately, we have had no real effort to develop the law with respect to the conduct of activities during the last 60 or 70 years, apart from the one accident, you might call it, which occurred at Geneva in 1925.

Let me discuss briefly several of the suggestions which I have made as part of the effort to fill the hiatuses which presently exist in the law of armed conflict with regard both to the conduct of hostilities and to the humanitarian or personnel area. I do not believe that my criticism of the existing law is based upon the fact that there is anything radically wrong with what we have on the books; rather it is based on the fact that we don't have on the books many laws that we should have, many laws that World War I, and World War II, and the many conflicts which have occurred since 1945, have demonstrated to be necessary.

My first proposal is headed "the need for a method for the automatic determination that a particular inter-State relationship requires the application of the law of armed conflict." Now, Mr. Schreiber has mentioned some of the difficulties encountered in this area. One of the 1907 Hague Conventions is concerned with the problem of the opening of hostilities, and it provides that a State must give a reasoned declaration of war, or an ultimatum with a time period; and that when war actually exists, neutral States must be so notified. That Convention was signed in 1907. In 1914 it was disregarded, notably right at the beginning of World War I, when Germany entered Belgium without a declaration of war.

Since 1914 the same disregarding of the 1907 Hague Convention has occurred on a number of occasions. Just a few examples: Italy attacked Ethiopia in 1935 without a declaration of war; Germany similarly attacked Poland in 1939; Russia attacked Finland that same year; and, of course, I do not have to remind you of Pearl Harbor. Not only were the provisions of the Third Hague Convention of 1907 disregarded on each of these, and many other occasions, but when that was called to the attention of the delinquent countries, they advanced a number of reasons for asserting that compliance had not been necessary. For example, Japan called its war against China in the late 1930s a "police action", insisting that there was no war and, if effect, that the law of war did not apply for that reason! And during World War II Germany had a number of excuses for its failure to apply the law of war in particular cases: that there was no legitimate government in existence with which it could be at war; that all of the enemy territory had been occupied and that there was, therefore, no country with which Germany could be at war; or that the enemy government had capitulated and that the government in exile was not a legitimate government; etc.

In order to remedy this situation, and to prevent its recurrence, the ICRC proposed the inclusion in Article 2 of each of the 1949 Conventions of a provision that the law contained in that Convention would be applicable, and I now quote, "to all cases of declared war" (an unusual situation these days) "or any other armed conflict which may arise between two or more of the High Contracting Parties, even if the state of war is not recognized by one of them." When that language was adopted without debate and without dissent at the 1949 Geneva Diplomatic Conference, it was felt that a great achievement had been attained, that this was *the* solution, that there would be no more episodes such as those to which I have just referred. Unfortunately, it has not worked out that way because we still do not have declarations of war, we still have the contention advanced that various types of armed conflict are not "war" and that, therefore, the law of war, the law of armed conflict, is not applicable. We still have parties like North

Vietnam and the Pathet Lao saying that the hostilities in which they are engaged are not war because there has been no declaration of war, and insisting that the 1949 Geneva Conventions are not applicable. Such a contention, of course, is directly contrary to the specific words of the Conventions and to the unambiguous intent of the draftsmen.

I say that there must be a solution, there must be some way that you can point the finger at a participant in hostilities and say, "You are engaged in armed conflict. This brings into operation the law of armed conflict. You must, for example, give prisoners of war and civilians the benefit of the 1949 Geneva Conventions to which you are a Party."

My proposed solution to this problem is not original. There were two suggestions made at the 1949 Diplomatic Conference which sought to deal with the problem in somewhat different ways. The first proposal, advanced by the Greek Government, would have had the Security Council of the United Nations determine if a state of belligerency existed. This proposal was dropped, but I do not think that it was a good one in any event because the Security Council is not going to make decisions based upon facts alone. Let us face it, the Security Council is a political organ, it is going to make decisions based upon politics, it is going to make decisions based upon the self interest of the member countries, and the representatives on the Council are going to vote strictly in accordance with instructions received from their Foreign Offices. So I do not believe that giving the authority, or the power, or the duty, to a political organ such as the Security Council would be an effective solution.

I come now to the second proposal made at the 1949 Diplomatic Conference, a proposal which was made in a somewhat different context. The French proposed the creation of an independent international body which would be available to act as a substitute for the Protecting Power in the event of the absence of such a Power. It would have been constituted of individuals of international stature, people who had previously been members of the International Court of Justice, people who had won Nobel Peace Prizes, people of all nationalities of that stature, people who would act as individuals and not as representatives of a country.

This proposal was not adopted. However, a resolution was adopted by the Conference recommending that consideration be given to the creation of such a body. As far as I have been able to determine, more than twenty years later no consideration has ever been given to it. Now I propose that it not only be considered but that, with appropriate modifications, it be adopted and that there be created a non-political organ which will determine, upon the application of any party to the convention which creates this organ, or of one of the parties to an armed conflict if the other party denies it, whether a state of "armed conflict" actually exists. That, of course, is the language of the Geneva Conventions; and if this proposed organ determines that a state of armed conflict does exist, then all of the parties to that armed conflict would be bound to apply all of the law of armed conflict, including both Hague law and Geneva law. Incidentally, like all bodies created in our era, it would have to have a name which would form an acronym. I have, therefore, called it the International Commission for the Enforcement of Human Rights during Armed Conflict—which becomes "ICEHRAC." I don't know what the connotations of this acronym are, but at least it is comparatively easy to say!

Now, I have an additional proposal, and that is that after a certain period of time, in the event that an investigation by this Commission discloses that one of the parties to this armed conflict is not complying with the law of armed conflict, the Commission will so declare. The convention creating the Commission will provide that, in the event of such a declaration of non-compliance with the law of armed conflict, there will be automatic sanctions against the non-complying country. I realize that the imposition of sanctions is an extreme measure. At the present time the only general treaty provision for the imposition of sanctions of which I am aware is that contained in the Charter of the United Nations, allocating that power to the Security Council. But I believe that sanctions of some kind, effective sanctions, are necessary so that a party to an armed conflict can be forced to comply with the applicable law, rather than waiting until the conflict is over and then punishing someone for not having complied with the law. By that time your civilians are dead, your prisoners of war are dead, and your people who have been injured or killed by illegal weapons have been injured or killed. So I propose that this Commission be given the very great power of declaring that there has been a failure to comply with the law of armed conflict and that, thereupon, without any further action on the part of the Commission, all the other parties to the new convention would be treaty-bound to impose the specified sanctions.

This is, of course, quite an idealistic proposal; and I am aware of the fact that, in these days of pragmatism, it will not be easy for some national leaders to absorb the proposal because of its apparent idealism. But what excuse can a state give if it is told that it is not complying with the law of armed conflict? Moreover, if it is believed that this provision for sanctions goes beyond the acceptable, and that it would be difficult to get wide ratification of a convention which contains such a provision, the convention would, of course, still be a complete and viable entity, even without the provision for sanctions. The latter is merely a method of attempting to ensure compliance with the law of armed conflict. Even without that provision, if the Commission had determined that a state of armed conflict existed, then the rest of the world would know that the law of armed conflict is supposed to be applied. If it were not applied, there would be a violation which would certainly not help the international public image of the country at fault, which would undoubtedly be seeking worldwide support. Unfortunately, there have been quite a few cases where public opinion has not been successful in acting as a stimulus to compliance, which is the basic reason for the sanctions proposal.

This, then, is my suggestion with respect to meeting the need for establishing a method by which it is to be determined that the law of armed conflict is applicable and should be applied. It is something that is not in existence at the present time, when we have a number of cases where, despite the fact that bullets are flying and bombs are dropping and people are being killed, the contention is made, and insisted upon, that there is no armed conflict and that the law of armed conflict is not applicable.

My second subject is concerned with another matter — the Protecting Power. The Protecting Power came into existence many centuries ago. It was entirely a creature of customary international law until a comparatively recent date, as a matter of fact, until the 1929 Geneva Prisoner-of-War Convention. That was the first multilateral convention which mentioned the Protecting Power. The Protecting Power, briefly, is a third country which acts behind the lines and within the territory of one belligerent for the protection of the personnel of the other belligerent. Under customary international law, if States A and B are at war, state A may select state C to be its Protecting Power. State B must then accept this selection before C may act as A's Protecting Power in the territory of B. Once A and B have agreed upon C, and C has accepted, then C, behind B's lines, acts as the Protecting Power for A, doing such things as visiting prisoner-of-war camps, to make sure that the provisions of the Geneva Conventions are being complied with.

The 1949 Geneva Conventions greatly expanded the duties of the Protecting Power and gave it a tremendous number of duties and a commensurate power, and also a staff to do the job. There is only one difficulty: there hasn't been a Protecting Power since 1945, either under the 1929 Geneva Convention until 1949 or under the 1949 Conventions since then! We have not had one armed conflict where there was such a third presence behind the lines or in the territory of the belligerents to ensure that the provisions of the 1949 Geneva Conventions were being carried out. Also, the Protecting Power as we know it today is established within the Geneva Convention framework so that the powers of the Protecting Power appear to be limited to the protection of personnel, prisoners of war, civilians, the sick and wounded. The Protecting Power appears to have no authority with respect to, and there is no method for the supervision of, conduct under the conduct-of-hostilities law, the Hague law. Again, while there is a provision in the 1949 Conventions for a substitute for the Protecting Power in the event that one has not been selected, no such substitute has ever been designated in accordance with such provision. This provision also provides that a humanitarian organization may offer its services as a substitute for the Protecting Power. The International Committee of the Red Cross has on many occasions, in fact on practically every occasion, offered its services for this purpose. In a number of cases this offer has been accepted. The International Committee of the Red Cross is still operating in Israel and in several of the Arab countries. It acted in Honduras and El Salvador in 1969 in order to accomplish the exchange of prisoners of war and to see that both sides were complying with the Geneva Conventions. The difficulties with which it was confronted in Nigeria in the purely humanitarian mission of trying to feed the population are well known.

Then you have another type of situation. It is the one which existed in Korea and now exists in Vietnam. The International Committee of the Red Cross immediately offered its services to both sides. This offer was accepted by South Korea; it was accepted by South Vietnam. It was not accepted by North Korea;

67

and it was not accepted by North Vietnam. Thus you have a third presence on one side but not on the other. That is a situation which calls for a remedy: first, to ensure the presence of the third party; and second, to extend the supervisory power of the Protecting Power to include the Hague Conventions, where conduct-of-hostilities law is involved.

Now, once again, ICEHRAC may be authorized to function to fill the void. I propose that when a decision is made, either by the parties themselves, or by ICEHRAC, that a state of armed conflict exists, the belligerents will select their own Protecting Powers in accordance with customary international law and the Geneva Conventions. However, if they fail to do so within a reasonable time, and in my proposal I have suggested one week, then ICEHRAC will automatically assume the functions of the Protecting Power on both sides. ICEHRAC would supervise compliance with both the 1949 Geneva Conventions and the law on conduct of hostilities. This would provide an impartial body, similar to the Swiss Government during World War II, which was accepted almost universally during that war because it was one of the few nations with the capability for performing this task and which remained neutral. The result was that in many cases Switzerland was the Protecting Power on both sides; and this worked tremendously to assist the Swiss in the performance of their task. If one side did not agree to act in a certain way, then they could expect that the other side was going to exhibit equal reticence in that particular regard. The desire for reciprocity will frequently work to get compliance on both sides.

The two matters which I have discussed, the determination that a state of armed conflict exists and a method of ensuring the existence of a third presence to oversee compliance with the law of armed conflict, are both more or less procedural in nature. My next two proposals are concerned with substantive matters. However, I shall not discuss my third proposal, which is concerned with biological and chemical weapons. I know that Congressman McCarthy is going to discuss that subject and I know that he and I think alike in this regard so that anything that he says will have my seconding. But I would like to cover briefly the last proposal that I have made. It deals with the use of air power.

It is a little difficult to realize, to accept the fact that, really, there is no law governing the use of air power in armed conflict. If we go back to 1907 once again, to the Hague Conventions, we find that there was one Declaration prohibiting the discharge of projectiles and explosives from balloons. It prohibited this activity not only from balloons, but also "by any other methods of a similar nature." That provision is our only basis for saying that there is any direct limitation on the use of air power in armed conflict. At that same time, however, one of the Conventions which was adopted prohibited bombardment "by whatever means" of inhabited places. Apparently the legislative history, the *travaux preparatoires*, indicate that when they included those words, the draftsmen were thinking of airplanes. Bear in mind that this was 1907. The Wright brothers had flown for the first time just three years before. No one then considered that the airplane would revolutionize warfare. However, its importance as a weapon was early recognized. A British Committee even made a report to the War Cabinet during World War I suggesting the possibility that the day would come when bombardment of the hitherto sacrosanct hinterland would be the method by which wars would be decided. World War II saw this type of bombardment become commonplace.

The Ninth Hague Convention of 1907, dealing with naval bombardments, had a provision which is also cited as indicating that there is existing law governing the use of air power. That provision excluded from the prohibitions on naval bombardments of undefended places certain specified military objectives. A naval vessel could not bombard an undefended place unless there was a specific military objective located in that place, such as an armament factory or a navy yard where shipping could be repaired. In the latter case the navy could bombard the military objective, even if it were located in an undefended place. This exception is of particular importance because the naval bombardment might well take place far behind the zone of land operations.

In World War I the airplane showed its potential. In 1922 there was a Conference held in Washington, and one of the things that Conference did was to establish a Committee of Jurists to study the problem of air warfare. That Committee met in The Hague in 1922 and 1923 and drafted a set of Rules of Air Warfare. Unfortunately, those Rules are still just a draft prepared by a small group of jurists many years ago. They were never adopted by anyone. And that was the major official attempt that has been made to establish a set of international rules governing the use of air power in combat.

I want to call to your attention two items contained in those Rules which are relevant to my proposal. First, they prohibited bombing which had as its objective the terrorizing of the civilian population or the injuring of noncombatants. Second, they limited air bombardment to specified military objectives in the zone of land operations, and then only if it gave a distinct military advantage and could be accomplished without the incidental bombing of civilians. Now this really means that they were attempting to limit air bombardment to tactical bombing in the zone of operations. Under these Rules the bombardment of the hinterlands which occurred during World War II would have been prohibited.

When World War II started, President Roosevelt and the Pope and a number of other world personages asked the belligerents for assurances that civilian noncombatants would not be subjected to bombing. They received these assurances; but it is estimated that twelve million civilians were killed by air bombardment! Mr. Schreiber mentioned that U.N. Document A/7720, the Secretary-General's "Report on Respect for Human Rights in Armed Conflict," proposes the use of safety zones for the protection of the civilian population; and he said that I considered these zones impractical. I suggest that you consider the case of the United States. Suppose that you were to establish a safety zone in this country. There would be well in excess of 100 million persons involved. The safety zone might have to be everything west of Pennsylvania and everything east of Idaho. This would include one-half to two-thirds of the territory of the United States. You cannot put that number of people in a zone 100 yards by 100 yards! The result is that in countries like the United States, or the U.S.S.R., or others having large populations and large land areas, it would require more than 50% of the total land area to receive all of the members of the civilian population who are noncombatants. I say that it is logistically impossible to move that number into the zone, and to take care of them there, and that no country could or would do it in time of war.

In addition, I don't care what kind of inspection system is devised, there will be violations of the safety zone. You are going to have important armaments made in the safety zone. You are going to have important armaments concealed in the safety zone. Inspectors can come and inspectors can go, and they will not find these hidden armaments; thus there will be an area of protected

70

unlawful activity. These are some of the reasons why I do not believe that the safety zone will work as a means of protecting the entire civilian population. The safety zone does have a valid purpose in the manner in which it has heretofore been conceived: that is, for such things as hospital safety zones, or zones for preganant women, or zones for small children, etc. But to say that you are going to take all of the noncombatants of a nation and put them in protected areas: I don't think that it can be done as a practical matter.

The International Committee of the Red Cross started working on this problem in the late Forties and early Fifties and presented to their Conference in New Delhi in 1956 a set of "Rules for the Protection of Civilian Persons in Time of War." These Rules, too, were impractical in many respects. They practically reached the point where a corporal would have had to determine, by paying a visit to the target, whether it would be a legitimate target! I don't think many corporals would enjoy such a task!

On the other hand, in the document which the I.C.R.C. prepared for its last Conference, entitled "Reaffirmation and Development of the Laws and Customs Applicable in Armed Conflict," the I.C.R.C has devloped a number of new principles. I think these principles are much more realistic. I have, therefore, borrowed from these principles, as well as from the 1923 Hague Rules, and from other sources, to establish my proposal with respect to strategic bombing, bombing of the hinterland far removed from the zone of land operations.

I first recommend the complete prohibition of terror bombing. I do not believe that there would be any debate or dispute on such a principle. I refer to an attack on the civilian population where there is no military target whatsoever, and where the attack is solely for the purpose of destroying the morale, the will to win, of that population. Almost every country has, at least for the record, said that it did not believe that terror bombing could ever be legal. The I.C.R.C. has found that such a practice is frequently counter-productive.

Secondly, I would prohibit target-area bombing. This is bombing where you have two or three targets in a large city and rather than spending the effort in trying to hit only those targets, you bomb the entire city. You are going to destroy those two or three targets in the city and accomplish your mission. Of course, you are also going to kill most of the civilians who live in the city — but that is just incidental; you did get your targets. In the Working Paper I mentioned that I was sure that technology had by now progressed to the point where it would be possible to bomb a target and just hit the target. Since preparing the proposal, I have seen a news item to the effect that the United States has now developed a laser-guided bomb which reduces the area of probable target error from 400 feet to ten feet. If it is now possible to bomb within ten feet of the target, I can see no need for target-area bombing to ensure the destruction of the target.

Finally, I would limit strategic bombing to military objectives. I believe that if you ban terror bombing, and if you ban target-area bombing, and if you require the use of the military objective as the standard for strategic bombing, you would have far fewer than the twelve million civilian dead of World War II.

Let me emphasize again that these are merely some proposals. I do not insist that they are the most serious inadequacies in the law of armed conflict. I do believe that conventions covering these areas would start us on the road to a more complete set of humanitarian rules to limit the effect of armed conflict. War is *per se* a period of killing—but at least we can try to limit the killing to combatants and we can limit the means of killing by restricting the use of certain weapons. These, in brief, are the objectives which my proposals seek to attain.

Introduction of Professor Richard Baxter

Our next speaker, Professor Richard Baxter, is well known to members of our Association and to lawyers interested in the study of international law. Professor Baxter has been a participant in past Hammerskjold Forums. After having graduated from Harvard Law School in 1948, he obtained the Diploma in International Law from Cambridge University in England. He served for a while in the office of the General Counsel of the Secretary of Defense, before joining the faculty of Harvard Law School in 1955. He has been a distinguished member of that faculty since then, becoming a full professor in 1959. In 1966 he returned to Cambridge University as a visiting professor for a year. In addition to teaching, Professor Baxter has devoted himself to many research projects in the field of international law and has authored several books and articles. He is a member of the Advisory Committee of the Institute of Air and Space Law of McGill University and has served with distinction as Vice-President of the American Society of International Law. He is currently a member of the Board of Editors of the American Journal of International Law. During World War II, Professor Baxter served in the U. S. Army, attaining the rank of Major and being awarded the Bronze Star. He is a retired Colonel of the U. S. Army Reserve. Professor Baxter brings to tonight's discussion an extensive knowledge of both the procedures and the substance of international law, as well as a willingness to propose new ideas for the development of international law.

Statement of Professor Baxter

I propose in the course of the next fifteen minutes to say a few words about the legal position of guerrillas and about the applicability of the law of war in civil conflict. These questions are timely and yet timeless.

In 1862, a professor of international law at Columbia College, Francis Lieber, persuaded General Henry Wager Halleck, then serving in a position comparable to that of the present-day Chief of Staff of the Army, to permit him to prepare a pamphlet on the legal position of guerrillas. This pamphlet, "Guerrilla Parties Considered with Reference to the Laws and Usages of War," was widely distributed to the Union forces and was of substantial assistance to them in dealing with this type of belligerent during our American Civil War. It remains today a most useful introduction to the law of guerrilla warfare.

It was during the American Civil War that there was also prepared the first modern codification of the law of war, General Orders No. 100, which came from the pen of this same Francis Lieber. This code, which regulated the conduct of the Union Forces, was widely adopted by other countries and helped to provide the impetus for the first international codifications of the law of war in the form of the Hague Regulations of 1899 and 1907.

Now, the problem of guerrilla warfare and the problem of the applicability of the law of war to civil conflict are, as you can well realize, not identical. But through the law regulating these two questions run several common threads of policy—that innocent civilians should be protected, that those who lay down their arms should likewise be put under the protection of international law, and that persons should not be allowed to assume the guise of innocent civilians as a cover for their belligerent activities.

73

Let us first turn to this problem as it arises in civil conflicts. The Geneva Conventions of 1949 attempted to deal with it in a novel way. Previous treaties on the law of war had not dealt with civil conflict at all. In the Conventions of 1949 there is one common article of the four Conventions, Article 3, which deals with "armed conflict[s] not of an international character." The Article begins

> In the case of armed conflict not of an international character occurring in the territory of one of the High Contracting Parties, each Party to the conflict shall be bound to apply, as a minimum, the following provisions:

There follows a very brief listing of the basic human rights of non-participants in the conflict and of persons who have engaged in hostilities but have laid down their arms.

There arises at the very outset a question as to when these provisions begin to have application. Characteristically, civil conflict may begin with a little bit of banditry or terrorism up in the hills. It may be very difficult to determine whether the shooting of government officials or policemen or bank officers or other affluent citizenry was done in order to enrich those who engaged in this pastime or whether those who engaged in this conduct were motivated by a serious political ideology. What later becomes the "glorious revolution" may start out as a bit of killing and looting, the throwing of a few hand grenades, and the picking off of a few unwary policemen. When is it then that a civil conflict in the terms of the Geneva Conventions of 1949 breaks out? I suppose that it must be at that time when there are too contending political factions, one of them the government, fighting it out, when the motive is no longer private gain but public good, and when each is in command of some territory. This is not specifically spelled out in the Conventions. The terms of Article 3 are such that both the lawful government and the rebels are bound to apply these provisions in a civil conflict on a basis of reciprocity. Of course, the rebels will be heard to ask why they, not being the government that signed the treaty, are obliged to carry out its provisions. The lawyer's response is that the rebels are bound *qua* nationals of the state that is a party to the treaties. But this will not make much sense to a political faction that is fighting against that very government that purported to assume the obligation on behalf of the state.

74

The next stage is reached when the two parties to a civil conflict can agree to apply the Conventions as a whole. There are again difficulties. First, agreement is needed between the two parties, and this may be difficult to achieve. The lawful government will not be favorably disposed toward treating with the rebels, and agreement between belligerents, regardless of their status, is never easy. Even if this agreement can be achieved, there is a problem about how one goes about applying the Conventions as a whole. There are elaborate provisions in the Geneva Civilians Convention of 1949 about occupied territory. Yet the occupied territory of civil conflict is actually liberated territory from the perspective of the belligerent that secures control of it. No government reasserting its control over an area which had previously been under the administration of rebels would say that it is "occupying" territory; it is "liberating" this territory from rebel control. It would be quite inappropriate in this situation to apply provisions that were designed to limit the powers of a belligerent in international conflict.

The other perplexing problem about the application of the Conventions as a whole to civil conflict is that it is very difficult to tell who is friend and who is enemy. In international conflicts, there are tests of enemy character such as service in the enemy armed forces, nationality, and residence. In civil conflicts, on the other hand, it is of the essence that one does not know whether the next person he meets is friend or enemy. Conventions designed to have application to enemy personnel, both military and civilian, do not comport well with conflicts in which both sides claim the loyalty of the populace as of right.

On top of this, civil wars are not purely domestic matters in these days. They usually have an international dimension as well. How does one determine, for example, whether the conflict in Vietnam is a civil conflict calling for the application in strict law only of the common Article 3 of the Geneva Conventions of 1949, or an international conflict to which all of the provisions of the Conventions are applicable? Does one examine the conflict as a whole? Does one look to the participation of a foreign state, such as the United States, as an indication that the war is international? Or does one look to each pair of belligerents? Does one say that in so far as the relation between South Vietnam and the Viet Cong is concerned, a civil war exists, but that the relationship between North Vietnam and the United States is such that there must be an international conflict between the two of them? And then there is the middle case—the hostilities between the forces of South Vietnam and those of North Vietnam. Is this conflict civil or is it international? And how does one, for example, distinguish a member of the Viet Cong, engaged in civil conflict, from a member of the North Vietnamese forces, participating in an international conflict? One immediately becomes entangled in legal niceties which are really not susceptible of application in the midst of war.

A further complication is that what starts out as a civil conflict may be, in the desire of the rebels, a prelude to an international conflict. This is the characteristic form of "wars of national liberation" and anti-colonialist wars. In such a case, the rebels do not desire to establish their paramountcy within one state but rather to free themselves from the control of that state and to establish a new sovereign and independent political unit. Thus, the position of Algeria was that it was declaring its independence from France, the colonial power. The Algerian Government was at pains to adhere to the Geneva Conventions of 1949 as early as possible in order to emphasize what it conceived to be the international character of the conflict. A civil conflict may thus escalate to an international conflict as the rebels gain their independence. But there will be no unanimity of characterization of the conflict, for the colonial power will continue to maintain that the conflict is a civil one, while the former colony will insist that the war has become international in character.

We must now turn to the problem of guerrillas. In civil conflicts as well as in certain forms of international conflicts there is an intermixing and mingling of combatants and non-combatants. The members of the armed forces who engage in combat may use civilians as a shield. Civilians may be held as hostages. The combatant may disguise himself as a civilian. He may engage in his occupation for part of the time, serving as a farmer by day and an assassin by night. Civilians themselves are often recruited to do violence to the opposing forces. A woman or a child, as veterans of the war in Vietnam can testify, may carry a hand grenade or plant a bomb. There has, especially in civil wars, been a willing intermingling of civilians with the combatants, and the combatants themselves have shown a certain disposition to hide under the cover of being peaceful civilians.

The criteria for determining whether a captured combatant is to be treated as a prisoner of war are set forth in Article 4 of the

76

Geneva Prisoners of War Convention. Most of the persons who engage in guerrilla warfare do not comply with these requirements. Consequently they are not entitled to treatment as prisoners of war upon capture and thus may, as an extreme measure, be punished with the penalty of death. The four requirements that must be met if combatants are to recognized as prisoners of war are that (1) they must be commanded by a person responsible for his subordinates (a requirement that guerrillas can satisfy); (2) they must carry a "fixed distinctive sign recognizable at a distance" (which not many guerrillas do); (3) they must carry arms openly (which guerrillas likewise often fail to do); and (4) they must conduct their operations in accordance with the laws and customs of war. If this last means giving proper care to their prisoners, they cannot, by the nature of their operations, carry out the provisions of the Geneva Prisoners of War Convention. Indeed, it is characteristic of a number of resistance movements in Africa that prisoners are routinely killed. According to a report in the *Economist,* the Zapu movement in Rhodesia, which is operating with the approval of the Organization of African Unity, kills its prisoners. The African National Congress in South Africa does likewise. Other resistance movements in Africa do not. It has been suggested that there could be certain technological break-throughs in the custody of prisoners by guerrillas which would permit them to carry about their captives in little wooden cages. But that too would not be in conformity with the Geneva Prisoners of War Convention of 1949.

Another respect in which guerrilla fighters do not comply with the law of war is that they often make attacks upon civilians. Civil conflict often starts out, as I have mentioned, with terrorism and sabotage, and this pattern often continues throughout the conflict. After all, the person who bicycles past a billet in Saigon and throws a bomb into it is engaging in hostilities against a legitimate military target in the form of enemy personnel, but a person who throws a grenade into the midst of a group of civilians commits a war crime by reason of his deliberate attack upon non-combatants. During the "confrontation" between Malaysia and Indonesia, saboteurs slipped into Singapore to bomb buildings. The people who planted these bombs, which killed and wounded civilians, were guilty of war crimes in having chosen the wrong targets for their violence. It is thus quite clear that most guerrilla fighters cannot now qualify for treatment as prisoners of war.

I now venture to suggest two possible solutions to these problems. First of all, as to civil wars, one article repeated in each of the four Geneva Conventions of 1949 is really not enough protection for combatants and non-combatants in what has become the characteristic form of contemporary warfare. What is needed is a new short convention dealing expressly with the protection of victims of civil conflicts. I say a *new* convention because it is unwise to attempt to alter the text of the existing Geneva Conventions of 1949. If changes were to be made in Article 3 itself, the door would be opened to what might turn out to be a complete revision of the Conventions. We would then have to repeat the whole dreary process of building up ratifications and accessions—a twenty year process, judged by experience with the Conventions of 1949—with states in the meanwhile being bound by inconsistent obligations.

The new convention on civil wars should take a human rights approach to the protection of war victims. One of the provisions might very well be that the death sentence should be suspended for the duration of a civil conflict, because the rebels of today may be the government leaders and heroes of tomorrow. There should be a precise definition of the level of domestic disorder at which the new convention would take effect. I suppose that it would remain true that the existing municipal law would be maintained in force and could be applied by the constituted government to the rebels. If new provisions could be worked out in some detail, that in itself would diminish the need to bring into force the Geneva Conventions as a whole, with all of the problems that their application would entail.

So far as guerrillas are concerned, it seems practicable to broaden the definition of those who are entitled to prisoner of war treatment and whose lives may therefore be spared. In Vietnam, the United States has gone beyond the terms of Article 4 of the Geneva Prisoners of War Convention and has extended prisoner of war treatment to members of Viet Cong main force units, even though they may not satisfy the four requirements that I read out to you. If it has proven possible to do this in the Vietnam conflict, there is good reason to suppose that this same broadening of eligibility for prisoner of war treatment might be attempted in both international and civil conflicts. That reform should be accompanied by a strict prohibition of, and prompt punishment for the acts of guerrillas who attack civilians or otherwise engage in war crimes. They would, of course, be treated as prisoners of war while being tried, to the extent they met the criteria of the broadened definition.

I cannot emphasize too strongly the importance of not disturbing the integrity of the Geneva Conventions of 1949 for the Protection of War Victims, which do represent the culmination of roughly a century of growth and increasing sophistication in the law of war. The Conventions have received widespread acceptance and have even been said by some to have passed into customary international law binding upon all nations, whether or not parties to the treaties.

These are my very modest proposals about how one might deal with these complex problems of the application of international law in civil conflicts and of the treatment to be accorded to guerrilla fighters.

Introduction of Congressman Richard D. McCarthy

Our final speaker this evening is Congressman Richard D. McCarthy of Buffalo, New York. Congressman McCarthy has a distinguished background in the public relations field and in public service. After graduating from Canisius College, he served as a reporter for the Buffalo Evening News before entering employment with the National Gypsum Company, for which he was Director of Public Relations for several years. Congressman McCarthy's interest in public affairs was already evident at that time, and he served as Vice-President of the Greater Buffalo Development Foundation from 1957 to 1963. He served with the United States Navy in the South Pacific in 1945 and 1946 and later with the United States Army in the Far East at the time of the Korean War. Since 1964 he has been the Representative in Congress of the 39th District of New York. In the House of Representatives he is a member of the Committee of Public Works and active on several sub-committees. He has recently declared himself a candidate for the United States Senate.

In the last few years Congressman McCarthy has given attention to the problem of chemical and biological warfare, a topic which is always referred to in ominous terms but about which very few persons have much knowledge. Congressman McCarthy has addressed himself to this issue several times in speeches on the floor of the House of Representatives. A book by Congressman

McCarthy was published in 1969 under the title "The Ultimate Folly, War by Pestilence, Asphyxiation, and Defoliation." I will quote one paragraph from the book at pages 27 and 28 to convey an impression of the horrors with which it deals:

> At Fort Detrick, workers don sterilized clothing and enter elaborate laboratories through an intricate system of air locks and ultraviolet rays to practice "public health in reverse." Research and development workers spend some $20 million a year producing such diseases as pneumonic plague, a more deadly version of the Black Death that killed a quarter of the human race in the Middle Ages; pulmonary anthrax, an often-fatal lung infection so tenacious that an area of Utah where it was tested in the 1950's probably will remain contaminated for a century; and botulism toxin, one ounce of which, effectively dispersed, could kill every human being in North America.

Statement of Congressman McCarthy

The United States is one of two major nations in the world which have not ratified the Geneva Protocol of 1925 banning chemical and biological warfare. This, in my view, is a serious omission because it remains as one of the few international laws which have effectively limited man's inhumanity to man. For more than four decades, from the last gun of World War I to the opening gun of the Vietnamese War, it worked, and no poison gas or germ warfare was used throughout this long period. There were a few exceptions, but they were brief and called forth the indignant protestations of mankind. Even the ferocious and long conflict of World War II did not include the use of poison gas or germ warfare. There were a number of reasons why this was so. Some credit international law, the Geneva Protocol. Others will say that it was the fear of retaliation that prevented the use of these weapons of mass destruction which destroy civilians as well as combatants. Certainly the public's horror and revulsion at weapons such as those cited by Mr. Carey from my book played a part in the prevention of the use of these weapons as did the attitude of key civilians and military leaders. My own opinion is that both legal and practical reasons were responsible for precluding the use of these weapons throughout that long period.

The question of ratification of the Geneva Protocol probably would never have arisen, for although we had not ratified it in 1925 when it was brought forward, every President from Calvin Coolidge until Dwight D. Eisenhower asserted that the United

States would not be the first to use chemical or biological weapons. Our policy was clear, or so it seemed anyway. Then, towards the end of President Eisenhower's second term there was a growing recognition in Congress and scientific circles that our policy was beginning to change. Our rearmament, started after the outbreak of the Korean War, included a major investment in chemical and biological warfare. There were a number of reasons for this: the acquisition by the United States military of the nerve gases produced by the Germans in World War II and new breakthroughs in biology and in other areas that prompted our military to begin serious investment in chemical and biological warfare weaponry. Then in 1959 and 1960 the U. S. Army made a concerted public effort to gain acceptability for chemical and biological warfare. They launched a major publicity drive with articles in Harper's, in the Atlantic and other publications citing chemical and biological weapons as a form of humane warfare. It was at that time that a Congressman, Representative Robert Kastenmeier of Wisconsin, introduced a resolution in the House of Representatives which restated the longstanding policy from Coolidge to Eisenhower that the U. S. would not be the first to use these weapons. The administration refused to support that resolution, it never came to a vote, and it was an ominous sign of what was to occur in a little country in Southeast Asia.

Our difficulties in fighting the war in Southeast Asia and the changes in technology that had occurred between the First World War and 1965 led to the first serious breakdown in the Geneva Protocol. Our massive use of the harassing gas, CS-2, and of plant-killing defoliants against both crops and vegetation are clearly, in my opinion, violations of the Protocol. It is not only my opinion but by a vote of 80 to 7 in the U.N. General Assembly it was declared that these two weapons are covered by the provisions of the Protocol. But it is the official position of the United States that these chemicals are not covered by the Geneva Protocol. In his introduction to his recent and excellent report on chemical and biological warfare, the Secretary General of the United Nations, U Thant, called on all nations to acknowledge that irritant gases, tear gas and others are covered by the Protocol. There is less of a specific nature that can be shown to include defoliants under the Protocol because they did not exist in 1925 when the Protocol was drafted. But I believe that they are covered in the prohibition against noxious chemicals, even if not identified specifically.

81

The issue of whether the so-called tear gases or irritant gases and defoliants are covered by the Protocol is central to a number of policy decisions that are before the President of the United States for action now and will be soon before the U. S. Senate. I share the opinion of those who believe that the Geneva Protocol will be seriously weakened if the United States attempts, as it would seem now, to exclude the so-called harassing gases and defoliants from the coverage of this Treaty. It is very possible that most of the nations that have signed the Protocol will not regard the United States as a signatory if we include reservations to permit the use of these two chemicals. And, we will certainly lose any benefits in the international community that might be gained by us by ratification if we attempt to exclude our massive chemical operations now being conducted in Vietnam. I cannot believe that other nations will not call into question our use of plant-killing chemicals in Vietnam, Laos, and Cambodia. I cannot believe that our massive use of CS-2 gas to help drive enemy troops into the open where they can be attacked with conventional weapons will be ignored by the Protocol signers.

Although in my opinion there is no question that tear gas was included in the Geneva Protocol, there are some groups who claim that it was not, and with some justification. Tear gas was not mentioned in the language of the Protocol, although Philip Noel-Baker, Nobel Peace Prize winner, member of the British Parliment, who was present at Geneva in 1925 recently declared in letters to the *New York Times* and the *London Times* that the drafters clearly had it in mind. Countries have always reserved the right to use tear gas of course for domestic disturbances and some have confused this use with its use in war. These factors and our initial use of newer forms of tear gas in combat in Vietnam without a top level policy decision have put us in a position where it is difficult for some in Washington to admit that these gases might be prohibited by the Protocol.

Similarly in the case of defoliants, initial decision to use plant-killing chemicals on a fairly small scale escalated without review and analysis so that we have defoliated an area in Vietnam roughly the size of Massachusetts. Aside from the massive scale of this chemical operation and its possible ecological damage to Vietnam, we have done so without the sort of military analysis that would tell us whether this defoliation is genuinely useful. Like so many programs, defoliation has an impetus of its own.

The best illustration is the use of defoliants along the Rung Sat Canal. Defoliants have been used to kill plant life on both sides of the 60-mile long Rung Sat Canal that leads from the sea to Saigon. The argument for the use of this defoliant is that its effects prevent attacks on ships in the Canal. Although no ships have been sunk in the Rung Sat Canal either before or after defoliation, the military argue that they cannot afford to have even one ship sunk. They go on, however, to point out that the Canal is only narrow enough to permit serious attack for about one kilometer. When questioned on this the military acknowledged that they really only need to defoliate for one kilometer but the broad-brush approach to decisions leads to the much wider and more destructive use of this chemical over 60 miles. As it is, we do not know whether defoliation is militarily effective, whether it is harmful to civilians, or whether it will permanently alter the characteristics of Vietnam.

You may have seen an article in yesterday's New York Times by Mr. Ralph Blumenthal which certainly ties in with the central theme of this discussion of "when battle rages, how can civilians be protected?" In the article, Mr. Blumenthal provides new data about the possible adverse genetic effects of the defoliant 2, 4, 5-T. He cites the cases of three mothers in villages in South Vietnam who believed that their deformed infants were deformed prior to birth by the fact that the mothers were exposed to the defoliant 2, 4, 5-T which had been sprayed in their area. This comes on the heels of a series of tests run at the Bionetics Laboratory in Bethesda Maryland under the sponsorship of the National Cancer Institute which show that this same defoliant 2, 4, 5-T is teratogenic, that is, it produces birth defects in test animals. This was so disturbing to the President's science advisor, Dr. Lee DuBridge, that on October 29 he announced that this defoliant would be banned in the United States and that its use would be restricted to unpopulated areas in Vietnam. That ban was not put into effect and the Pentagon announced the following day that they would continue to use it in training and regroupment areas which, of course, are populated. This prompted me to take the floor of the House of Representatives today to again urge that the use of this be halted until it can be shown that it is not teratogenic to human beings.

I am also informed that no studies have been made of the effectiveness of the harassing or tear gases in warfare in Vietnam.

We have the subjective opinions of some military after they have used it in combat, but we do not have the type of weapons analysis that usually precedes the adoption of any new weapon. One of the few studies that have been made on the use of tear gas was done by the Rand Corporation and pointed out that civilians were particularly vulnerable to injury when tear gas is used, since it drives them out of their protective shelters into the line of rifle or artillery or B52 fire. This is certainly a far cry from the justification that we have used it in the past to limit casualties.

I believe that there is a workable solution to the question now facing the White House of whether the tear or harassing gases and defoliants are covered by the Protocol. Although I believe that they are covered, I suggest that the question be left open for now when the Protocol is submitted to the Senate for ratification. In doing so the Administration will have an opportunity to determine on an objective basis whether or not there is a military value to these chemicals. We may also find, hopefully, that our involvement in Vietnam has staged down sufficiently so that decisions on the use of tear gas and defoliants are no longer caught up in the immediate pressures of the war.

Delaying a decision on tear gas and defoliants would also give us time to see if the General Assembly votes next November to ask for an advisory opinion from the International Court of Justice on the applicability of the Protocol to tear gas and defoliants. There is a good possibility as I understand it that the General Assembly will vote to ask for such an opinion next November. If it does so, and the International Court of Justice rules that tear gas and defoliants are prohibited by the Geneva Protocol, it would jeopardize all the efforts that have gone into ratification of the Geneva Protocol by the United States if we had in the Senate excluded those two chemicals. We would have to start all over again, and our experience suggests that on the second try we might not be successful. We most remember that the wording of this protocol was ratified by the Senate in 1922 but in three years lobbying efforts were launched by the chemical industry, by veterans' groups and the army and when it came up again in 1925, it was never approved, and that is why we remain to this day a non-signatory.

It is particularly distressing that those who have discussed the Geneva Protocol at the top policy level in our Government have, to my knowledge, not considered alternatives open to them in dealing with the tear gas and defoliant issues. By attempting to come up with a definitive policy at this time they are closing out an opportunity for progress, a chance to exert some leadership in setting a standard of international behavior. Because of the position that they are taking thus far, the United States is involved in trying to convince other nations to modify their stands on tear gas and defoliants. Our diplomatic pressures have been applied to support a position that would seem not tenable.

Although overshadowed by nuclear clouds, chemical warfare still remains a weapon of mass destruction and should be eliminated from the arsenals of man. If we are successful in abandoning biological warfare, as President Nixon announced in November, and in ratifying the Protocol, perhaps we can then move on to a verifiable system, when the technology exists, that would permit us to abandon chemical weapons, including defoliants and irritant gases in war. In view of the marginal military effectiveness of these weapons, I believe that we might succeed in this effort.

Comments by Professor R. Q. Quentin-Baxter, Faculty of Law, Victoria University of Wellington, and Representative of New Zealand in the United Nations Commission of Human Rights.

I have three comments—but I intend them interrogatively, in case they should evoke a different view from a member of the panel.

It is axiomatic that all legislation in this field must be within limits set by the reasonable needs of military security. At the Geneva Conference of 1949 there were intensive efforts to probe those limits and to provide maximum protection—especially for civilians in occupied territory. Delegates experienced in the demands of warfare and in the hazards faced by civilian populations were convinced that the area of protection afforded by the Geneva Conventions could be greatly extended.

As far as I know, there was—despite the record of aerial and other bombing of centres of population in the Second World War—no corresponding belief that greater protection could be given in areas appropriate to the Hague Conventions. I think that this difference is significant, and that the reasons for it would still obtain to-day. No doubt more can and must be done to regulate the use of weapons—for example, chemical and bacteriological weapons—whose military effectiveness is imponderable; but, apart from that, it would seem that the best hope of progress lies in improving the application of the Geneva Conventions.

Secondly, did the 1949 Conventions achieve a realistic balance between the aim of protecting war victims and the demands of military security? There is certainly some evidence that the requirements of the Conventions have been considered unwieldy in conflicts of a limited and localised character. I would therefore respectfully agree with Professor Baxter's conclusion that the pressing need is not for the revision of the 1949 Conventions, but for the establishment of a supplementary treaty which makes simpler provision for armed conflicts of a limited character.

Finally, is there any factor other than considerations of military advantage which may impede the application of the Geneva Conventions? I think one must acknowledge that there is—at least in relation to conflicts of an internal character. Governments faced with an insurrection see very strong political objection in conceding belligerent status to insurgents. This is surely the context in which it may be most useful to draw upon the human rights tradition—which has no experience of tempering its standards to meet the demands of military security, but which does seek to bind governments in their relations with their own subjects. Even so, the matter is bound to be one of great delicacy.

SELECTED BIBLIOGRAPHY

Selected Bibliography on
The Laws of War As They Affect the
Individual

Prepared by Anthony P. Grech
Librarian, The Association of the Bar
of the City of New York

General

Academy of Sciences of the U.S.S.R., Institute of State and Law. International law. Moscow, Foreign Languages Pub. House. 1957? (Chap. 10, Law and customs of war, pp. 401-54)

Atlay, J. B. Legitimate and illegitimate modes of warfare. 1905. 6 J. Soc'y Comp. Legis. (n.s.) 10-21.

Baker, Joseph R. and Crocker, Henry G. The laws of land warfare concerning the rights and duties of belligerents as existing on August 1, 1914. Washington, Gov't Print. Off. 1919. 420p.

Baker, Joseph R. and McKernan, Louis W. Selected topics connected with the laws of warfare as of August 1, 1914. Washington, Gov't Print. Off. 1919. 851p.

Balladore Pallieri, G. Diritto bellico. 2d. ed. Padova, Cedam. 1954. 464p.

Ballis, William. The legal position of war: changes in its practice and theory from Plato to Vattel. The Hague, Nijhoff. 1937. 184p.

Barclay, Thomas (Sir). Law and usage of war: a practical handbook of the law and usage of land and naval warfare and prize. London, Constable & Co. 1914. 245p.

Baty, Thomas and Morgan, J. H. War: its conduct and legal results. London, J. Murray. 1915. 578p.

Baxter, Richard R.
Forces for compliance with the rules of war (followed by comments by Benjamin Forman, Gordon B. Baldwin and Howard S. Levie). 1964. 58 Am. Soc'y Int'l L. Proc. 82-99.
The role of law in modern war. 1953. 47 Am. Soc'y Int'l L. Proc. 90-98.
The role of law in modern war (in Gross, Leo., ed. International law in the twentieth century. N. Y., Appleton-Century-Crofts, 1969, pp. 658-66)

Belli, Pierino. De re militari et bello tractatus. Oxford, Clarendon Press. 1936. 2v. [Vol. I, Photographic reproduction of the edition of 1563 . . . Vol. 2, Translation "A treatise on military matters and warfare" (trans. by) Herbert C. Nutting]

Berber, F. Lehrbuch des völkerrechts. 2.bd: kriegsrecht. München, Beck. 1962. 312p.

Bishop, William W., jr. International law. 2d ed. Boston, Little, Brown. 1962. [Chapter 8, Force and war, pp. 744-901]

Bivens, William J. Restatement of the laws of war as applied to the armed forces of collective security arrangements. 1954. 48 Am. J. Int'l L. 140-45.

Borchard, Edwin M. International law of war since the war. 1934. 19 Iowa L. Rev. 165-76.

Bordwell, Percy. The law of war between belligerents. Chicago, Callaghan. 1908. 374p.

Bothe, M. Le droit de la guerre et les Nations Unies. Genève, Droz. 1967.

Brand, George. The development of the international law of war. 1951. 25 Tul. L. Rev. 186-204.

Brownlie, Ian. International law and the use of force by states. Oxford, Clarendon Press. 1963. 532p.

Busquets Bragulat, J. Etica y derecho de guerra. 1966. 31 Rev. Española de Derecho Militar 81-94.

Cansacchi, G. Nozioni di diritto internazionale bellico. Torino, Giappichelli. 1963. 176p.

Carnegie, A. R. Jurisdiction over violations of the laws and customs of war. 1963. 39 Brit. Yb. Int'l L. 402-24.

Castel, J. G. International law chiefly as interpreted and applied in Canada. Toronto, Univ. of Toronto Press. 1965. [State and effects of war, pp. 1112-1206]

Castrén, Erik Johannes Sakari. The present law of war and neutrality. Helsinki. 1954. 630p.

Commission of Jurists to Consider and Report Upon the Revision of the Rules of Warfare. General report (In International commission for the revision of the rules of warfare . . . Despatch from the first British delegate, 1924, pp. 4-60)

Compliance during hostilities: a panel—forces for compliance with the law of war. R. R. Baxter: comments; B. Forman, G. B. Baldwin, H. S. Levie: discussion. 1964. 58 Am. Soc'y Int'l L. Proc. 82-99.

Constantopoulos, D. Les raisons de la crise du droit de la guerre. 1956. Jahrbüch für Internationales Recht 22-33.

Coursier, Henri.
  Définition du droit humanitaire. 1955. 1 Ann. Français de Droit International 223-27.
  L'évolution du droit international humanitaire (In Hague Academy of international law. Recueil des cours 1960, 1, vol. 99, pp. 357-461)

Cowles, Willard B. Recent practical aspects of the laws of war. 1943. 18 Tul. L. Rev. 121-40.

Delbez, Louis. Les principes généraux du droit international public. Paris. Pichon et Durand-Auzias. 1963. [Book 3, Le droit de la guerre, pp. 507-600]

Deltentre, Marcel, ed. Recueil général des lois et coutumes de la guerre, terrestre, maritime, sous-marine et aérienne, d'après les actes élaborés par les conférences internationales depuis 1856 . . . Bruxelles, F. Wellens-Pay. 1943. 885p.

Downey, William Gerald. The law of war and military necessity. 1953. 47 Am. J. Int'l L. 251-62.

Dunbar, N. C. W.
  The legal regulation of modern warfare. 1955. 40 Grotius Soc'y 83-95.

The significance of military necessity in the law of war. 1955. 67 Jurid. Rev. 201-12.

Edmunds, Sterling E. The laws of war: their rise in the nineteenth century and their collapse in the twentieth. 1929. 15 Va. L. Rev. 305-49.

Fauchille, Paul. Traité de droit international public. Paris, Librairie Arthur Rousseau. 1921. [Vol. 2, Guerre et neutralité]

Fedozzi, Prospero. Trattato di diritto internazionale, in collaborazione di vari autori, per cura di Fedozzi e Santi Romano. Padova, Cedam, Casa editrice dott. A. Milani. [Vol. III, La guerra di Giorgio Balladore Pallieri, 1935, 478p.]

Fenwick, Charles G. International law. 3d ed. rev. and enl. New York and London, Appleton-Century-Crofts. [Chap. 29, Laws of land and aerial warfare, pp. 552-82]

Field, David Dudley. Amelioration of the laws of war required by modern civilization. 1887. 36 Albany L.J. 284-88.

François, J. P. A.

Légalite d'application des règles du droit de la guerre aux parties à conflit armé. 1963. 50 (1) de l' Institut de Droit International 5-127.

Reconsidération des principes du droit de la guerre. 1957. 47 (1) Ann. de l' Institut de Droit International 323-606; 1959. 48 (2): 178-263.

Fratcher, William F. The new law of land warfare. 1957. 22 Mo. L. Rev. 143-61.

Friedmann, Wolfgang. International law and the present war. 1940. 3 Modern L. Rev. 177-94.

Gabaglia, A. C. Raja. Guerra e direito international. São Paulo, Saraiva. 1949. 637p.

Garner, James Wilford.

The German war code; a comparison of the German manual of the laws of war with those of the United States, Great Britain and France and with the Hague convention respecting the laws and customs of war on land. Urbana, Ill., Pub. by the University under the direction of the War Committee. 1918.

International law and the world war. London, Longmans, Green. 1920. 2v.

Les lois de la guerre, leur valeur, leur avenir. 1936. 17 Rev. de Droit International et de Législation Comparé (3d series) 96-117.

The outlook for the law of war and of neutrality. 1936. 22 Grotius Soc'y 1-12.

Gentili, Alberico. De iure belli libri. Oxford, Clarendon Press. 1933. 2v. [Vol. 1, Photographic reproduction of the edition of 1612; Vol. 2 The translation of the edition of 1612 by John C. Rolfe, "The law of war"]

Giraud, Emile. Le respect des droits de l' homme dans la guerre internationale et dans la guerre civile. 1958. 74 Rev. du Droit Public 613-75.

Gómez, Calero, J. Los fundamentales derechos humanos y su protección jurídica en caso de conflicto armado. 1969. 36 Rev. General de Derecho 923-33.

Greenspan, Morris.

The modern law of land warfare. Berkeley, Univ. of California Press. 1959. 724p.

The soldier's guide to the laws of war. Washington, Public Affairs Press. 1969. 87p.

Grob, Fritz. The relativity of war and peace, a study in law, history and politics; foreword by Roscoe Pound. New Haven, Yale Univ. Press. 1949. 402p.

Grotius, Hugo. Hugonis Grotii de jure belli ac pacis libri tres, in quibus jus naturae & gentium, itme juris publici praecipua explicantur. Edito nova cum annotatis anctoris ex postrema ejus ante obitum cura multo nunc auctior. Accesserunt & annotato in Epistolam Pauli ad Philemonem. Washington, Carnegie Institution of Washington. 1913-25. 2v. [V.1, Reproduction of the edition of 1646. V.2, The translation of book 1 by Francis W. Kelsey, with the collaboration of Arthur E. R. Boak, Henry A. Sanders, Jesse S. Reeves and· Herbert F. Wright, and an introduction by James Brown Scott]

Guggenheim, Paul; Traité de droit international public. Genève, Georg. 1953. 2v. [Vol. 2, chap. 5, Le droit de la guerre, pp. 295-492]

Hackworth, Green Haywood. Digest of international law. Washington, Gov't Print. Off. 1943. [Vol. 6, chap XX, War]

Higgins, Alexander P. War and the private citizen; studies in international law. London, P. S. King & Son. 1912. 200p.

Human rights, the laws of war and armed conflicts. 1968. 35 Bull. Int'l Comm'n Jurists 3-12.

Hyde, Charles C. International law chiefly as interpreted by the United States. Boston, Little, Brown. 1945. [Vol. 3, Title G, Land warfare, pp. 1792-1913]

Jessup, Philip C. Political and humanitarian approaches to limitation of warfare. 1957. 51 Am. J. Int'l L. 757-61.

Joyce, James Avery. Red Cross international and the strategy of peace. New York, Oceana. 1959. 270p.

Juristentagung, 2d Vienna, 1962. Vorträge gehalten von J. S. Pictet, und J. P. Schoenholzer auf der 2 Juristentagung veranstaltet von der Osterreichischen gesellschaft vom Roten Kreuz, Wien 18-19 Marz, 1962. 23p.

Kunz, Josef Laurenz.

The chaotic status of the laws of war and the urgent necessity for their revision. 1951. 45 Am. J. Int'l L. 37-61.

La crise et les transformations du droit des gens (in Hague. Academy of international law. Recueil des cours 1955, 11, vol. 88, pp. 1-104)

Kriegsrecht im all gemeinen (In Wörterbuch des völkerrechts. Berlin, Gruyter, 1961, vol. 2, pp. 354-59)

The laws of war. 1956. 50 Am. J. Int'l L. 313-37.

The new U.S. army field manual on the law of land warfare. 1957. 51 Am. J. Int'l L. 388-96.

Plus de lois de la guerre? 1934. 41 Rev. Générale de Droit International Public 22-57.

La problemática actual de leyes de la guerra. Valladolid. 1955. 164p.

Lachs, Manfred. The unwritten laws of warfare. 1945. 20 Tul. L. Rev. 120-28.

Kelsen, Hans. Principles of international law. 2d ed. revised and edited by Robert W. Tucker. New York, Holt, Rinehart & Winston. 1962. (pp. 87-154)

Lapradelle, Albert Geouffre de and Dehousse, Fernand. La reconstruction du droit de la guerre . . . analyses, documents, projets. Paris, Les Editions Internationales; Bruxelles, E. Bruylant. 1936. 147p.

Lapradelle, Paul Geouffre de. Le côntrole de l' application des conventions humanitaires en cas de conflit armé. 1956. 2 Ann. Français de Droit 343-52.

Lauterpacht, Hersh.
The limits of the operation of the law of war. 1953. 30 Brit. Yb. Int'l L. 206-43.
The problem of the revision of the law of war. 1952. 29 Brit. Yb. Int'l L. 360-82.

Lawrence, T. J. The effect of the war on international law (in Grotius Society. Problems of the war . . . London, Sweet & Maxwell, 1917, vol. 111, pp. 105-15)

Laws of war. 1949 Yb. Int'l L. Comm'n 281.

The League of Nations and the laws of war. 1920-21 Brit Yb. Int'l L. 109-24.

Leguey-Feilleux, J. R. The law of war: a bibliography 1945-1958. 1960. 2 World Polity 319-412.

McDougal, Myres S. and Feliciano, Florentino P.
International coercion and world public order: the general principles of the law of war. 1958. 67 Yale L. J. 771-845.
Law and minimum world public order; the legal regulation and international coercion. New Haven, Yale Univ. Press. 1961. 872p.

McDougal, Myres S. and others. Studies in world public order. New Haven, Yale Univ. Press. 1960. 1058p.

Manner, George. The legal nature and punishment of criminal acts of violence contrary to the laws of war. 1943. 37 Am. J. Int'l L. 407-35.

Marin Luna, Miguel A. The evolution and present status of the laws of war (In Hague. Academy of international law. Recueil des cours 1957, 11, Leyden, vol. 92, pp. 629-754)

Moore, John Bassett. A digest of international law. Washington, Gov't Print. Off. 1906. [Vol. 7, secs. 1100-65]

Moynier, Gustave. Essai sur les caractères généraux des lois de la guerre. Gènève, C. Eggiman. 1895. 120p.

Oppenheim, L. International law. 7th ed. by H. Lauterpacht. London, Longmans, Green. 1952. [Vol. 2, Disputes, war and neutrality]

Paris. Peace Conference, 1919. *Commission on the Responsibility of the authors of the war and on enforcement of penalties.* Violation of the laws and customs of war; reports of majority and dissenting reports of Americans and Japanese members of the commission. . . . Oxford, Clarendon Press; New York, H. Milford. 1919. [For the Carnegie endowment for international peace, Division of international law]

Phillipson, Coleman. International law and the great war. London, T. Fisher Unwin. 1915. 407p.

Pictet, Jean Simon.
The development of international humanitarian law (In Jenks, C. W. International law in a changing world. Dobbs Ferry, N.Y., Oceana, 1963, pp. 114-25)
The laws of war. Talks given on June 15 and 22, 1960, in the lecture series

of the International radio university. Geneva. 1961. 11p.

The need to restore the laws and customs relating to armed conflicts. 1969. 9 Int'l Rev. Red Cross 459-78.

The principles of international humanitarian law. 1966. 6 Int'l Rev. Red Cross 455-69, 511-33, 587-91.

The principles of international humanitarian law. Geneva, International Committee of the Red Cross. 1967. 62p.

The XXth international conference of the Red Cross: results in the legal field. 1966. 7 Int'l Comm'n Jurists J. 3-19.

Pillet, Antoine. La guerre et le droit. Louvain, A. Uystpruyst-Dieudonné. 1922. 158p.

Pinto, Roger. Les règles du droit international concernant la guerre civile (In Hague. Academy of international law. Recueil des cours 1965, 1, vol. 114, pp. 455-548)

Reconsidération des principes du droit de la guerre. 1959. 11 Ann. de l'Institut de Droit International 178-263.

Red Cross. International Committee, Geneva.

Handbook of the International Red Cross; conventions, statutes and regulations, resolutions of the international conference of the Red Cross and of the Board of governors of the league of Red Cross societies. 10th ed. Geneva. 1953. 615p.

Reaffirmation and development of the laws and customs applicable in armed conflicts. Report. Geneva. 1969. 79p.

Redslob, Robert. Traité de droit des gens. Paris, Sirey. 1950. pp. 306-47.

Risley, John Shuckbaugh. The law of war. London, A. D. Innes. 1897. 307p.

Rolin, Albéric. Le droit moderne de la guerre. Les principes, les conventions. Les usages et les abus. Bruxelles, A. Dewit. 1920-21. 3v.

Röling, B. V. A. The law of war and the national jurisdiction since 1945 (In Hague. Academie de droit international. Recueil des cours 1960, 11, vol. 100, pp. 325-456)

Rousseau, Charles. Droit international public. Paris, Sirey. 1953. (pp. 537-734)

Ruegger, Paul. L'organisation de la Croix-Rouge internationale sous ses aspects juridiques (In Hague. Academy of international law. Recueil des cours 1953, 1, vol. 82, pp. 375-585)

Saksena, Kunar Chandra. Public international law. 3d ed., rev. & enlarged. Allahabad, Central Law Agency. 1960. [Part III, Laws of war, pp. 645-754]

Sastry, K. R. R. Studies in international law. Calcutta, Eastern Law House Ltd. 1952. [B-war, pp. 237-325]

Schwarzenberger, Georg.

From the laws of war to the law of armed conflict. 1968. 21 Current Leg. Prob. 239-58; 1968. 17 J. Pub. L. 61-77.

Functions and foundations of the laws of war (In Patna university. Patna law college. Studies in law. Bombay, 1961, pp. 78-102)

Functions and foundations of the laws of war. Oct. 1965. 1 (2-4) Civ. & Mil. L. J. 31-49.

International law as applied by international courts and tribunals. London, Stevens. 1968. [Vol. 2, The law of armed conflict]

A manual of international law. 5th ed. New York, Praeger. 1967. (pp. 196-236)

Neo-barbarism and international law. 1968. Yb. World Aff. 191-213.

Sereni, Angelo Piero.
Diritto internazionale. Milano, Giuffrè. 1965. Vol. 4.
Ragione di guerra e principi di umanità nel diritto internazionale bellico. 1964. 47 Riv. di Diritto Internazionale 169-85.

Sierra, Manuel J. Tratado de derecho internacional público. 2d ed. Mexico, Porrua. 1955. [Sexta parte, Guerra y neutralidad, pp. 451-510]

Société Internationale de Droit Pénal Militaire et de Droit de la Guerre, 2. Congrès Florence, 1961. L'aéronef militaire et le droit des gens: subordination et coopération militaire internationale. Strasbourg. 1963. 465p.

Spaight, James M. War rights on land. London, Macmillan. 1911. 520p.

Starke, J. G. An introduction to international law. 5th ed. London, Butterworths. 1963. [The "laws of war," pp. 416-28]

Stone, Julius. Legal controls of international conflict; a treatise on the dynamics of disputes and war-law. 2d impression, rev. with supplement 1953-1958. New York, Rinehart. 1959. 903p.

Taubenfeld, Howard J. International armed forces and the rules of war. 1951. 45 Am. J. Int'l L. 671-79.

United Nations. General Assembly. Respect for human rights in armed conflicts. Report of the Secretary-general. New York. 114p. [A/7720, 20 Nov. 1969]

United Nations. International Conference on Human Rights Teheran, 22 April to 13 May 1968. Final act. New York, United Nations. 1968. [Human rights in armed conflict, p. 18]

U.S. Laws, Statutes, etc. The law of land warfare. Washington. 1956. 236p. [Its Field manual FM27-10]

U.S. Naval War College. International law documents . . . 1894-1896, 1899-date. Washington, Gov't Print. Off. 1894-date. (title varies)

Verdross, Alfred. Völkerrecht. 5.neubearb. Wien, Springer. 1964. pp. 439-80.

Verraes, Fernand. Droit international. Les lois de la guerre et la neutralité. Bruxelles, O. Schepens. 1906. 2v.

Visscher, Charles de. Theory and reality in public international law. Princeton, Princeton Univ. Press. 1957. pp. 286-307.

Whiteman, Marjorie M. Digest of international law. Washington, Gov't Print. Off. 1968. Vols. 10 & 11.

Wilson, Robert R. Standards of humanitarianism in war. 1940. 34 Am. J. Int'l L. 320-24.

Woetzel, Robert K. Legal aspects of military uses of space in Soviet and American eyes (In Taubenfeld, Howard J., ed. Space and society. Dobbs Ferry, N.Y., Oceana, 1964, pp. 121-39)

Wright, Quincy.
The outlawry of war and the law of war. 1953. 47 Am. J. Int'l L. 365-76.
A study of war. 2d ed., with a commentary on war since 1942. Chicago, Univ. of Chicago Press. 1965. 2v.

Lieber Code - 1863

Baxter, R. R. The first modern codification of the law of war: Francis Lieber and general order no. 100. 1963. 3 Int'l Rev. Red Cross 171-89, 234-50.
Davis, George B.
Doctor Francis Lieber's instructions for the government of armies in the field. 1907. 1 Am. J. Int'l L. 13-25.
Memorandum showing the relation between general order no. 100 and the Hague convention with respect to the laws and customs of war on land. 1913. 7 Am. J. Int'l L. 466-69.
Francis Lieber (In Root, Elihu. Addresses on international subjects. Cambridge, Harvard univ. press, 1916, pp. 89-103)
Lieber, Guido Norman. Leyes de la guerra, instrucciones del doctor Lieber para el ejército en campaña. Mexico, J. S. Ponce de Leon. 1871. 40p.
Nys, Ernest. Francis Lieber—his life and his work. 1911. 5 Am. J. Int'l L. 117, 355-93.
Root, Elihu. Francis Lieber. 1913. 7 Am. J. Int'l L. 453-66.
Sallet, R. On Francis Lieber and his contribution to the law of nations of today (In Gottlinger Arbeitskreis. Recht im dienste der menschenwürde, festschrift für Herbert Kraus. Würzburg, 1964, pp. 279-306)
Shepard, W.S. One hundreth anniversary of the Lieber code. 1963. (27-100-21) Mil. L. Rev. 157-62.

Geneva Convention - August 22, 1864

Gillot, Louis. La révision de la convention de Gèneve au point de vue historique et dogmatique. Paris, A. Rousseau. 1902. 370p.
Lueder, Carl Christoph J. F. L. La convention de Genève au point de vue historique, critique et dogmatique . . . ouvrage qui a remporté le prix offert en 1873 par S. M. l'impératrice d'Allemagne; tr. par les soins du Comité international de la Croix-Rouge. Erlangen, E. Besold. 1876. 414p.

Moynier, Gustave.
Étude sur la convention de Genève pour l'amélioration du sort des militaires blessés dans les armées en campagne (1864 et 1868). Paris, J. Cherbuliez. 1870. 376p.
La convention de Genève pendant la guerre franco-allemande. Gèneve, Soullier & Wirth. 1873. 58p.

Brussels Conference - 1874

Actes de la conference de Bruxelles (1874). Bruxelles, F. Hayez. 1874. 311 p.
Conférence de Bruxelles. Projet d'une convention internationale concernant les lois et coutumes de la guerre. (Texte primitif soumis a la conférence.) Projet d'une declaration internationale concernant les lois et coutumes de la guerre. (Texte modifié par la conference.) Protocoles des séances, plénières de la conférence. Protocoles des séances de la commission déleguée par la conférence. Annexes. La Haye. 1890.
Correspondence respecting the conference at Brussels on the rules of military

warfare; supplement to the London Gazette, Oct. 24, 1874.
Dakin, Winthrop S. Index to the proceedings of the Brussels conference on the rules of military warfare, 1874. (n.p., 194?)

Mechelynck, Albert, ed. La convention de La Haye concernant les lois et coutumes de la guerre sur terre, d'après les actes et documents des conférences de Bruxelles de 1874 et de La Haye de 1899 et 1907. Grand, A. Hoste. 1915. 465p.
Project of an international declaration concerning the laws and customs of war adopted by the conference of Brussels, Aug. 27, 1874. 1 Am. J. Int'l L. Supp. 96-103.
The Russian congress on the laws of war, at Brussels in 1874. 1874. 9 Am. L. Rev. 193-211.

Hague. International Peace Conference - 1899

The Hague conventions and declarations of 1899 and 1907, accompanied by tables of signatures, ratifications and adhesions of the various powers and texts of reservations; ed. by James Brown Scott, director. New York, Oxford Univ. Press. 1915. 303p.
The Hague convention of 1899 (11) and 1907 (IV) respecting the laws and customs of war on land. Washington, The Endowment. 1915. 33p. (Carnegie endowment for international peace, division of international law, pam. no. 5)
The Hague conventions of 1899 (III) and 1907 (X) for the adaption to maritime warfare of the principles of the Geneva convention. Washington, The Endowment. (Carnegie endowment for international peace, division of international law, pam. no. 6)
The Hague declaration of 1899 (IV, I) and 1907 (XIV) prohibiting the discharge of projectiles and explosives from balloons. Washington, The Endowment. 1915. 5p. (Carnegie endowment for international peace, division of international law, pam. no. 7)
The Hague declaration (IV, 2) of 1899 concerning asphyxiating gases. Washington, The Endowment. 2p. (Carnegie endowment for international peace, division of international law, pam. no . 8)
The Hague declaration (IV, 3) of 1899 concerning expanding bullets. Washington. The Endowment. 1915. 2p. (Carnegie endowment for international peace, division of international law, pam. no. 9)
The final acts of the first and second Hague peace conferences. Washington, The Endowment. 1915. 40p. (Carnegie endowment for international peace, division of international law, pam. no. 10)
The proceedings of the Hague peace conferences; translation of the official texts, prepared in the division of international law of the Carnegie endowment for international peace under the supervision of James Brown Scott, director. New York, Oxford Univ. Press. 1920-21. 5v.
The reports to the Hague conferences of 1899 and 1907; being the official explanatory and interpretative commentary accompanying the draft conventions and declarations submitted to the conferences by the several commissions charged wtih preparing them together with the texts of the

final acts, conventions and declarations as signed, and of the principal proposals offered by the delegations of the various powers as well as of other documents laid before the commissions; ed., with an introduction by James Brown Scott. Oxford, Clarendon Press; London, New York, H. Milford. 1917. 940p.

Bordin, Paul. Les lois de la guerre et les deux conférences de la Haye (1899, 1907). Paris, A. Pedone. 1908. 282p.

Choate, Joseph H. The two Hague conferences. Princeton, Princeton Univ. Press. 1913. 109p.

Daehne van Varick, August von. Documents relating to the program of the first Hague peace conference laid before the conference by the Netherlands government. Translation. Oxford, Clarendon Press. 1921. 115p.

Davis, Calvin DeArmond. The United States and the first Hague peace conference. Ithaca, N.Y., Published for the American Historical Society by Cornell Univ. Press. 1962. 236p.

Ferguson, Jan H. The international conference of the Hague; a plea for peace in social evolution. The Hague, Nijhoff. 1899. 107p.

Higgins, Alexander P. The Hague peace conferences and other international conferences concerning the laws and usages of war. Texts of conventions with commentaries. Cambridge, The University Press. 1909. 632p.

Holls, Frederick W. The peace conference at the Hague, and its bearings on international law and policy. New York, Macmillan. 1900. 572p.

Hull, William I. The two Hague conferences and their contributions to international law. Boston, For the International School of Peace, Ginn & Co. 1908. 516p.

Mechelynck, Albert, ed. La convention de la Haye concernant les lois et coutumes de la guerre sur terre, d'après les actes et documents des conférences de Bruxelles de 1874 et de la Haye de 1899 et 1907. Gand, A. Hoste. 1915. 465p.

Mérignhac, Alexandre Giraud J. A.
La conférence internationale de la paix; étude historique, exégétique et critique des travaux et des résolutions de la conférence de la Haye de 1899. Paris, A. Rousseau. 1900. 460p.
Les lois et coutumes de la guerre sur terre d'après le droit international moderne et la codification de la conférence de la Haye de 1899. Paris, A. Chevalier-Maresq. 1903. 412p.

Pillet, Antoine.
Les conventions de la Haye du 29 juillet 1899 et du 18 octobre 1907; étude juridique et critique. Paris, A. Pedone. 1918. 274p.
Les lois actuelles de la guerre. 2 éd. contenant: la texte commenté des conventions de la Haye du 29 juillet 1899 touchant les lois de la querre sur terre et sur d'adaptation de la convention de Genève aux guerres maritimes. Paris, A. Rousseau. 1901. 504p.

Scott, James Brown.
Instructions to the American delegates to the Hague peace conferences and their official reports. New York, Oxford Univ. Press. 1916. 139p.
The Hague peace conferences of 1899 and 1907. Baltimore, Johns Hopkins Press. 1909. 2v.

Stead, William T. La chronique de la conférence de la Haye 1899.

Accompagné du texte de conventions. Paris, La Haye, J. Hockstra. 1901. 2v.

Geneva. *Conference for Revision of the Geneva Convention of 1864, 1906*

Conferencia internacional de Ginebra, 11 de junio de 1906, celebrada con objeto de perfeccionar y completar la convención firmada en aquella ciudad el 22 agosto de 1864, para mejorar la suerte de los heridos y enfermos de los ejércitos en campaña. Mexico, Secretaría de Guerra y Marina, Talleres del Departamento de Estado Mayor. 1909. 54p.

Convention de Genève; actes de la conférence de révision réunie à Genève du 11 juin au 6 juillet 1906. Genève, Imprimerie H. Jarrys. 1906. 310p.

The Geneva convention of 1906, for the amelioration of the condition of the wounded in armies in the field. Washington, The Endowment. 1916. 17p. (Carnegie endowment for international peace, division of international law, pam. no. 23)

Delpech, Joseph. La nouvelle convention de Genève (6 juillet 1906) pour l'amélioration du sort des blessés & malades dans les armées en campagne. Paris, A. Pedone. 1907. 104p.

Lemoine, Albert. Les conventions internationales sur le régime des prisonniers de guerre. Conférence da la Haye. Convention de Genève; leur application dans la guerre actuelle. Paris, L. Tenin. 1917. 76p.

Wehberg, Hans, ed. Die abkommen der Haager friedenskonferenzen, der Londoner seekriegskonferenz nebst Genfer konvention. . . . Neue ausg., enthaltend den stand der ratifikationen und beitrittserklärungen vom 1. März 1915. Berlin, J. Guttentag. 1915. 270p.

Hague. *International Peace Conference 2nd 1907*

Convention between the United States and other powers respecting the laws and customs of war on land. Signed at the Hague Oct. 18, 1907. Washington, Gov't Print. Off. 1910. 40p.

The Hague convention (III) of 1907 relative to the opening of hostilities. Washington, The Endowment. 1915. 4p. (Carnegie endowment for international peace, division of international law, pam. no. 12)

The Hague convention of 1899 (II) and 1907 (IV) respecting the laws and customs of war on land. Washington, The Endowment. 1915. 33p. (Carnegie endowment for international peace, division of international law, pam. no. 5)

The Hague convention (V) of 1907 respecting the rights and duties of neutral powers and persons in case of war on land. Washington, The Endowment. 1915. 8p. (Carnegie endowment for international peace, division of international law, pam. no. 13)

The Hague conventions of 1899 (III) and 1907 (X) for the adaption to maritime warfare of the principles of the Geneva convention. Washington, The Endowment. 1915. (Carnegie endowment for international peace, division of internation law, pam. no. 6)

The Hague declaration of 1899 (IV, I) and 1907 (XIV) prohibiting the discharge of projectiles and explosives from balloons. Washington, The Endowment. 1915. 5p. (Carnegie endowment for international peace, division of international law, pam. no. 7)

The Hague conventions and declarations of 1899 and 1907, accompanied by tables of signatures, ratifications and adhesions of the various powers, and texts of reservations; ed. by James Brown Scott, director. New York, Oxford Univ. Press. 1915. 303p.

The proceedings of the Hague peace conferences; translation of the official texts, prepared in the division of international law of the Carnegie endowment for international peace under the supervision of James Brown Scott, director. New York, Oxford Univ. Press. 1920-21. 5v.

The reports to the Hague conference of 1899 and 1907; being the official explanatory and interpretive commentary accompanying the draft conventions and declarations submitted to the conferences by the several commissions charged with preparing them, together with the texts of the final acts, conventions and declarations as signed, and of the principal proposals offered by the delegations of the various powers as well as of other documents laid before the commissions; ed. with an introd. by James Brown Scott. Oxford, Clarendon Press; London, New York, H. Milford. 1917. 940p.

Barclay, Thomas (Sir).

International law and practice, with appendices containing the Hague conventions of 1907, Declaration of London 1909 (with drafting committee's report) and materials converning branches therefore susceptible of adjustment on the termination of the war. London, Sweet & Maxwell. 1917. 316p.

The second Hague conference; memorandum on controverted questions of international practice, suggested reforms, etc. London. 1906. 159p.

Bellot, Hugh H. L. War crimes: their prevention and punishment (In Grotius society. Problems of war. . . . London, Sweet & Maxwell, 1917, v. II, pp. 31-55)

Boidin, Paul. Les lois de la guerre et les deux conférences de la Haye (1899-1907). Paris, A. Pedone. 1908. 282p.

Bustamente y Servén, Antonio Sánchez de. La seconde conférence de la paix, réunie à la Haye en 1907. Paris, L. Larose et L. Tenin. 1909. 765p.

Choate, Joseph H. The two Hague conferences. Princeton, Princeton Univ. Press. 1913. 109p.

Conventions and declarations between the powers concerning war, arbitration and neutrality. The Hague, Nijhoff. 1915. 135p.

Davis, George B. The amelioration of the rules of war on land. 1908. 2 Am. J. Int'l L. 63-77.

Higgins, Alexander P. The Hague peace conferences and other international conferences concerning the laws and usages of war. Texts of conventions with commentaries. Cambridge, The University Press. 1909. 632p.

Hull, William I. The two Hague conferences and their contributions to international law. Boston, For the International School of Peace, Ginn & Co. 1908. 516p.

Mechelynck, Albert, ed. La convention de la Haye concernant les lois et coutumes de la guerre sur terre, d'après les actes et documents des conférences de Bruxelles de 1874 et de la Haye de 1899 et 1907. Gand, A.

Hoste. 1915. 465p.

Meurer, Christian. Die Haager friedenskonferenz. München, J. Schweitzer Verlag. 1905-07. 2v.

Scott, James Brown.
The Hague peace conferences of 1899 and 1907. Baltimore, Johns Hopkins Press. 1909. 2v.

Instructions to the American delegates to the Hague peace conferences and their official reports. New York, Oxford Univ. Press. 1916. 139p.

The work of the second Hague peace conference. 1908. 2 Am. J. Int'l L. 1-28.

Geneva. Conference for Revision of the Geneva Convention of 1906, 1929

Acte final de la conférence diplomatique convoquée pour la révision de la convention de Genève du 6 juillet 1906 pour l'amélioration du sort des blessés et malades dans les armées en campagne et pour l'élaboration d'une convention relative au traitement des prisonniers de guerre. Du 27 juillet 1929. Genève, Impr. du Journal de Genève. 1930. 18p.

Actes de la conférence diplomatique convoquée par le conseil fédéral suisse pour la révision de la convention du 6 juillet 1906 pour l'amélioration du sort des blessés et malades dans les armées en campagne et pour l'élaboration d'une convention relative au traitement des prisonniers de guerre et réunie à Genève du 1ᵉʳ au 27 juillet 1929. Genève, Impr. du Journal de Genève. 1930. 771p.

Amelioration of the condition of the wounded and the sick of armies in the field (Red Cross convention). Convention between the United States of America and other powers. Signed at Geneva, July 27, 1929. Proclaimed by the president of the United States, Aug. 4, 1932. Washington, Gov't Print. Off. 1932. 37p. (Treaty series no. 847)

Conférence diplomatique convoquée pour la révision de la convention de Genève du 6 juillet 1906 pour l'amélioration du sort des blessés et des malades dans les armées en campagne et pour l'élaboration d'une convention relative au traitement des prisonniers de guerre (juillet 1929). Acte final. 10p. (n.p., n.d.)

Conférence diplomatique pour la révision de la convention de Genève et l'élaboration d'une convention internationale relative au traitement des prisonniers de guerre (1ᵉʳ-5ᵐᵉ séance plénière, 1ᵉʳ au 27 juillet 1929). Genève. (n.d.) 5 pts.

Convention de Genève pour l'amélioration du sort des blessés et des malades dans les armées en campagne. Du 27 juillet 1929. Genève, Impr. du Journal de Genève. 1930. 28p.

Convenzione internazionale sul trattamento dei prigionieri di guerra. (Gazzetta ufficiale del regno d'Italia, n. 243 del 16 ottobre 1940-XVIII, Gior. mil. uff. 1940, circolare 795, disp. 53 del 31 ottobre 1940-XIX) Roma, Istituto Poligrafico dello Stato, Libreria. 1941. 50p.

Deuxième commission. Code des prisonniers de guerre. 3ᵐᵉ séance, 4-25 juillet 1929. Genève. (n.d.) 8pts.

International convention relative to the treatment of prisoners of war. Geneva, July 27, 1929. Ottawa, F. A. Acland, Printer to the King. 1931. 31p.

International convention for the amelioration of the condition of the wounded and sick in armies in the field. Geneva, July 27, 1929. [The convention has not been ratified by His Majesty] London, H. M. Stat. Off. 1931. 47p. (Cmd. 3793)

Première commission. Révision de la convention de Genève. 1er-21me séance, 2-26 juillet 1929. Genève. (n.d.) 21 pts.

Prisoners of war. Convention between the United States of America and other powers. Signed at Geneva, July 27, 1929. Proclaimed by the president of the United States, Aug. 4, 1932. Washington, Gov't Print. Off. 1932. 66p. (Treaty series no. 846)

Bakker, H. De conventie van Genève van 27 juli 1929 tot verbetering van het lot van gewonden en zicken in de legers de velde. Ultgegeven door het hoofdbestuur van het nederlandsche Rovde Kruis. 1931. 96p.

Cresson, W. P. A new convention regarding prisoners of war. 1930. 24 Am J. Int'l L. 148-51.

Des Gouttes, Paul. La convention de Genève pour l'amélioration du sort des blessés et des malades dans les armées en campagne du 27 juillet 1929. Préface de Max Huber. Genève, Comité International de la Croix-Rouge. 1930. 267p.

Flynn, Eleanor C. The Geneva convention on treatment of prisoners of war. 1943. 11 Geo. Wash. L. Rev. 505-20.

Garner, James W. Recent conventions for the regulation of war. 1932. 26 Am. J. Int'l L. 807-11.

Waltzog, Alfons, ed. Recht der landkriegsführung, die wichtigsten abkommen des landkriegsrechts. Berlin, F. Vahlen. 1942. 304p.

Geneva. Convention of 1949

Diplomatic Conference for the Establishment of International Conventions for the Protection of Victims of War, Geneva, 1949.

Actes de la conférence diplomatique de Genève de 1949. Berne, Département Politique Fédéral. 1950? 2v. in 3.

Acte final. Final act. Geneva. 1949. 15p.

CDG/Bless/Art. Clauses common to all four conventions, etc. 1-52, June 24-July 4, 1949. Geneva.

CDG/Bless/CR. Comm. I. Convention on the sick and wounded. Summary record of the meeting, 1st. April 25, 1949. Geneva.

CDG/CIV. Civilians convention. Text adopted, amendments, etc. 1-5888, April 25-July 19, 1949. Geneva.

CDG/CIV/Art. Clauses common to all conventions. Draft of article adopted by committee III, etc. 1-40; June 24-July 4, 1949. Geneva.

CDG/CIV/CR.Comm. III. Civilian convention. Summary record of the meeting, 1st. April 25, 1949. Geneva.

CDG/Mix/CR. Joint committee: clauses common to all four conventions. Summary record of the meeting 1st—April 26, 1949—Geneva.

CDG/NAUF. Comm. I. Maritime convention. Amendment 1st—April 23, 1949—Geneva.

CDG/NAUF/Art. Comm. I. Maritime warfare convention 1st—June 24, 1949—Geneva.

Convention de Genève pour l'amélioration du sort des blessés des malades et des naufragés des forces armées sur mer du 12 août 1949. Geneva convention for the amelioration of the condition of wounded, sick and shipwrecked members of armed forces at sea of 12 Aug. 1949. Geneva. 1949. 38p.

Convention de Genève pour l'amélioration du sort des blessés et des malades dans les forces armées en campagne du 12 août 1949. Geneva. 1949. 44p.

Convention de Genève relative à la protection des personnes civiles en temps de guerre du 12 août 1949. Geneva. 1949. 61p.

Les conventions de Genève du 12 août 1949. 2. éd. Genève. 1950. 251p.

Les conventions de Genève du 12 août 1949. Commentaire, publié sous la direction de Jean S. Pictet. Genève, Comité International de la Croix-Rouge. 1952.

Conventions de Genève pour la protection des victimes de la guerre. (n.p.) 1951. 199p.

Conventions for the protection of war victims, Geneva, Aug. 12, 1949. London, H. M. Stat. Off. 1958. 361p. (Cmnd. 550)

Delegation from Denmark. Beretning. Kobenhavn. 1950. 24p.

Final act of the conference for the revision of the Geneva convention of 27th July 1929 for the relief of the wounded and sick in armies in the field, of the Xth Hague convention of 18th Oct. 1907 for the adaptation to maritime warfare of the principles of the Geneva convention of 1906 and of the convention concluded at Geneva on 27th July, 1929 relative to the treatment of prisoners of war; and for the establishment of a convention relative to the protection of civilian persons in time of war, with resolutions, conventions and annexes. Geneva, 21 April to 12 Aug. 1949. London, H. M. Stat. Off. 1950. 146p. (Cmd. 8083)

Final record. Berne, Federal Political Department. 195–. 3v. in 4.

The Geneva convention of Aug. 12, 1949. 2d rev. ed. Geneva. 1950. 245p.

Geneva conventions of Aug. 12, 1949 for the protection of war victims. Washington, Gov't Print. Off. 1950. 255p. (Gen. for. pol. ser. 34)

Geneva conventions of Aug. 12, 1949 for the protection of war victims. Washington, Gov't Print. Off. 1950. 270p. (Gen. for. pol. ser. 34)

Die Genfer Rotkreuz—abkommen vom 12. August 1949 sowie das abkommen betreffend die gesetze und gebräuche des landkrieges vom 18. Oktober 1907 und anlage (Haager landkriegsordnung). Mit einer einführung von Dr. Anton Schlögel. 3. erweiterte aufl. Mainz, Hüthig und Dreyer. 1955. 302p.

Protection of war victims, armed forces at sea. Convention, with annex, between the United States of America and other governments, dated at Geneva Aug. 12, 1949. Washington, Gov't Print. Off. 1956. 99p.

Protection of war victims, armed forces in the field. Convention, with annexes, between the United States of America and other governments, dated at Geneva Aug. 12, 1949. Washington, Gov't Print. Off. 1956. 104p.

Protection of war victims, civilian persons. Convention, with annexes, between the United States of America and other governments, dated at

Geneva Aug. 12, 1949. Washington, Gov't Print. Off. 1956. 181p.
Résolutions. Geneva. 1949. 4p.
Die vier Genfer abkommen zum schutze der opfer des krieges vom 12. 8.
1949. Englischer und deutscher von Dr. Franz Groh. Frankfurt am
Main, A. Metzner. 1954. 160p.
Alonso, J. S. The Geneva convention (In Conference on world peace through
law. 2d. Washington, D.C., 1965. Building law rules and legal institutions
for peace. St. Paul, West, 1967, pp. 600-08)
American Bar Association. Sec. of International and Comparative Law.
Comm. on Military, Naval and Air Law. The Geneva conventions of 1949.
A lectured prepared by the committee. (n.p., n.d.) 14p.
Arean, B. A. Convenio de Ginebra relativo al trato de prisioneros de guerra
(1949). Consideraciones sobre sus principales articulos. Buenos Aires,
Universidad Nacional, Facultad de Derecho y Ciencias Sociales. Lecciones
y Ensayos (No. 29). 1965. (pp. 85-102)

Aureglia, L. et Lapradelle, P. de. Organisation, fonctionnement et protection
du contrôle de l'application des conventions humanitaires en cas de conflits armés. 1958. 2 Annales de Droit International Médical 47-70.
Bartos, M. and Patrnogic, J. Droit international humanitaire dans le monde
contemporain. 1964. 10 Annales de Droit International Medical 17-23.
Braun, Ulrich. Die anwendung der Genfer zivilkonventionion in kriegen
nicht-internationalen charakters. Winterthut, P. G. Keller. 1962. 130p.
Cilleuls, J. des. Plan of action for the dissemination of the Geneva conventions. 1965. 5 Int'l Rev. Red Cross 64-70.

Commission of Government Experts for the Study of Conventions for the
Protection of War Victims. Rapport sur les travaux de la conférence
d'experts gouvernementaux pour l'étude des conventions protégeant les
victimes de la guerre (Genève 14-26 Avril 1947). Geneva, Comité Inter-
national de la Croix-Rouge. 1947. 355p.
Coursier, Henri.
Course of five lessons on the Geneva conventions. Geneva, International
Committee of the Red Cross. 1963. 102p.
Les principes de la convention de Genève. 1959. 41 Rev. Internationale de
la Croix-Rouge 487-98.
Dillon, J. V. The genesis of the 1949 convention relative to the treatment of
prisoners of war. 1950. 5 Miami L.Q. 40-63.
Dissemination of the Geneva conventions among medical personnel. 1965. 5
Int'l Rev. Red Cross 171-81.
Draper, G. I. A. D.
The Geneva conventions of 1949 (In Hague. Academy of international
law. Recueil des cours 1965, I, vol. 114, pp63-162).
The Red Cross conventions. New York, Praeger. 1958. 228p.
Enomoto, Juji. Japan and the Geneva conventions of 1949. 1961. 5 Japanese
Ann. Int'l L. 15-24.
Esgain, Albert J. and Solf, Waldemar A. The 1949 Geneva convention relative
to the treatment of prisoners of war: its principles, innovations and de-
ficiencies. 1963. 41 N.C.L. Rev. 537-96.

Evard, E. Legal protection of aero-medical evacuation in war-time. 1966. 6 Int'l Rev. Red Cross 343-61.

Groh, Franz. Das recht kriegsgefangenen und zivilpersonen nach den Genfer konventionen vom 12.8. 1949. Unter besonderer berücksichtigung des erweiterten. Anwendungsbereicks und der verstarkten schutzbestimmungen des kriegsgefangenenabkommens. Hamburg. 1952. 145p.

Gutteridge, Joyce A. C. The Geneva conventions of 1949. 26 Brit. Yb. Int'l L. 294-326.

Hingorani, R. C. An appraisal of the Geneva convention (1949) relating to prisoners of war. 1964. 16 Law Rev. (Punjab Univ.) 17-53.

Hooker, Wade S., jr. and Savasten, David H. The Geneva convention of 1949; application in the Vietnamese conflict. 1965. 5 Va. J. Int'l L. 242-65.

A hundred states are now parties to the Geneva conventions. 1964. 4 Int'l Rev. Red Cross 312-16.

Implementation and dissemination of the Geneva convention of 1949. 1966. 6 Int'l Rev. Red Cross 640-44; 1965. 5:227-42.

Kruse-Jense, Carl. Traits dominants de la convention de Genève relative à la protection des personnes civiles en temps de guerre du 12 août 1949 (In Legal essays; a tribute to Frede Castberg. Copenhagen, 1963, pp. 262-79)

Lapradelle, Paul Geouffre de. La conférence diplomatique et les nouvelles conventions de Genève du 12 août, 1949. Paris, Editions Internationales. 1951. 423p.

Mandò, Alfredo. Gli aspetti etico-sociali e medico-sociali delle convenzioni di Ginevra del 12 agosto 1949. Chieti, C. Marchionne. 1958. 20p.

Netherlands. Departement van Buitkenlandsche Zaken. Diplomatieke conferentie voor de nieuwe Rode kruis verdragen, Genève, 21 April-12 Augustus 1949. 's-Gravenhage, Staatsdrukkerij-en Uitgeverijbedrijf. 1951. 423p. (Its Uitgaven no. 24)

Nó, Louis E. de. La garantía de los derechos individuales en el convenio de Ginebra sobre trato de prisioneros de guerra. 1964. 3 Rev. de Droit Pénal Militaire et de Droit de la Guerre 499-510.

On the Geneva convention relative to the treatment of prisoners of war. 1964. 4 Int'l Rev. Red Cross 202-07.

Patrnogic, J. Control of the application of humanitarian conventions. 1966. 5 Rev. de Droit Pénal Militaire et de Droit de la Guerre 405-15.

Pictet, Jean Simon.
  La croix-rouge et les conventions de Genève (In Hague. Academie de droit international. Recueil des cours 1950, I, vol. 76, pp. 1-118)
  Le droit international et l'activité du comité international de la croix-rouge en temps de guerre. Zürich, Orell Füssli Verlag. 1945. 54p.
  Geneva convention for the amelioration of the condition of the wounded and sick in armed forces in the field . . . with contributions by Frédéric Siordet and others. Geneva, International Committee of the Red Cross. 1952. 406p.
  Geneva convention for the amelioration of the condition of wounded, sick and shipwrecked members of armed forces at sea . . . by Pictet with the co-operation of Rear-Admiral M. W. Mouton, Frédéric Siordet and others. Geneva, International Committee of the Red Cross. 1960. 320p.

The new Geneva conventions for the protection of war victims. 1951. 45 Am. J. Int'l L. 462-75.

Pilloud, C. Reservations to the 1949 Geneva conventions. 1965. 5 Int'l Rev. Red Cross 343-50.

Red Cross. International Committee, Geneva.
Draft revised or new conventions for the protection of war victims, established by the international committee of the Red Cross with the assistance of government experts, national Red Cross societies and other humanitarian associations. Geneva. 1948. 245p.

The Geneva conventions of August 12, 1949. Analysis for the use of national Red Cross societies. Geneva. 1950. 2v.

The Geneva convention of 12 August 1949. Commentary published under the general editorship of Jean S. Pictet. Geneva. 1952-60. 4v.

Geneva convention relative to the treatment of prisoners of war. Geneva. 1960. 763p.

Preliminary documents submitted to the commission of government experts for the study of conventions for the protection of war victims, Geneva, April 14 to 26, 1947. Geneva. 1947. 3v.

Projets de conventions revisées ou nouvelles protégeant les victimes de la guerre, etablis par le comité international de la Croix-Rouge avec le concours d'experts des gouvernements, des sociétés nationales de la Croix-Rouge et d'autres associations humanitaires. Genève. 1948. 245p.

Projets de conventions, revisées ou nouvelles protégeant les victimes de la guerre: remarques et propositions. Document destiné du gouvernements invités par le conseil fédéral suisse à la conférence diplomatique de Genève, 21 avril 1949. Geneva. 1949. 49p.

Rapport sur les travaux de la conférence d'experts gouvernementaux pour l'étude des conventions protégeant les victimes de la guerre (Genève, 14-26 avril 1947). Genève. 1947. 355p.

Report on the work of the conference of government experts for the study of the conventions for the protection of war victims (Geneva, April 14-26, 1947). Geneva. 1947. 332p.

Report on the work of the preliminary conference of national Red Cross societies for the study of the conventions and various problems relative to the Red Cross, Geneva, July 26-Aug. 3, 1946. Geneva. 1947. 143p.

Revised and new draft conventions for the protection of war victims. Texts approved and amended by the XVIIth international Red Cross conference. Rev. translation. Geneva, Imprimerie du Journal de Genève. 1948.

Revised and new draft conventions for the protection of war victims. Remarks and proposals submitted by the international committee of the Red Cross. Geneva. 1949. 95p.

Schlögel, Anton. Genfer abkommen zum schutze der kriegsopfer vom 12.8. 1949 (In Wörterbuch des völkerrechts. Berlin, Gruyter, 1961, vol. 1, pp. 644-51)

Schmid, J. H. Die völkerrechtliche stellung der partisanen im kriege unter besonderer berucksichtigung des persönlichen geltungsbereiches der Genfer konventionen zum schutze der kriegsopfer vom 12 August 1949. Zurich, Polygraphischen Verlag. 1956. 196p.

Schneider, Peter. Internationales komitee vom Roten Kreuz (In Wörterbuch des völkerrechts. Berlin, Gruyter, 1961, vol. 2, pp. 125-27)

Seeger, Roland. Le statut personnel des étrangers ennemis et la convention de Genève du 12 août 1949 relative à la protection des civils. Zofingue, Editions Ringier. 1958. 166p.

Smith, Delbert D. The Geneva prisoner of war convention: an appraisal. 1967. 42 N.Y.U. L. Rev. 880-914.

U.S. Congress. Senate. Comm. on Foreign Relations.
Geneva conventions for the protection of war victims. Hearings . . . 84th cong. 1st sess. on executives D, E, F and G, 82d cong., 1st sess., the Geneva conventions for the protection of war victims, opened for signature at Geneva on Aug. 12, 1949. June 3, 1955. Washington, Gov't Print. Off. 1955. 68p.

Geneva conventions for the protection of war victims; report on executives D, E, F, and G, 82d cong., 1st sess. Washington, Gov't Print. Off. 1955. 32p.

U.S. Department of the Army. Lectures on the Geneva conventions of 1949. Washington. 1958. 25p. (Its pam. 20-151)

Urner, Paul. Die menschenrechte der zivilpersonen im krieg gemäss der Genfer zivilkonvention von 1949. Winterthur, P. G. Keller. 1956 151p.

Yingling, Raymund T. and Ginnane, Robert W. The Geneva conventions of 1949. 1952. 46 Am. J. Int'l L. 393-427.

Aerial Warfare

Aerial warfare and international law. 1942. 28 Va. L. Rev. 516-27.

Bordwell, Percy. Bombardment of residential districts. 1913. 20 Case & Comment 88-91.

Bosly, H. L'aéronef militaire et la protection de la vie humaine (In Société internationale de droit pénal militaire et de droit de la guerre. 2. Congrès, Florence, 1961 . . . L'aéronef militaire et le droit des gens: subordination et coopération militaire internationale, pp. 71-88, Strasbourg, 1963)

Bouruet-Aubertot, J. Les bombardements aériens. Paris, Les Presses Universitaires de France. 1923. 102p.

Cohn, Ernst M. Documents on the origins of international air law. 1967. 27 Fed. B.J. 314-24.

Colby, Elbridge.
Aerial law and war targets. 1925. 19 Am. J. Int'l L. 702-15.
Laws of aerial warfare. 1926. 10 Minn. L. Rev. 123-48, 207-34, 309-24.

De Nó, Louis E. y Tardio, P. R. La aeronave militar y los paises no participantes en la guerra (In Société internationale de droit pénal militaire et de droit de la guerre, 2. Congrès, Florence, 1961. L'aéronef militaire et le droit des gens: subordination et coopération militaire internationale, pp. 163-73, Strasbourg, 1963)

Garner, James W.
International régulation of air warfare. 1932. 3 Air L. Rev. 103-26, 309-23.
Proposed rules for the regulation of aerial warfare. 1924. 18 Am. J. Int'l L. 56-81.

La réglementation internationale de la guerre aérienne. Paris. 1923. 30p.

Gérard, C. Les bons offices des non-belligérants pour le respect des règles limitant les bombardements aériens (In Société internationale de droit pénal militaire et de droit de la guerre. 2. Congres, Florence, 1961. L'aeronef militaire et le droit des gens: subordination et coopération militaire internationale, pp. 192-98, Strasbourg, 1963)

Goda, P. J. Protection of civilians from bombardment by aircraft: the ineffectiveness of the international law of war. 1966. 33 Mil. L. Rev. 93.

Gosnell, Harpur Allen. Hague rules of aerial warfare. 1928. 62 Am. L. Rev. 409-29.

Henry-Couannier, André. Légitimité de la guerre aérienne. Paris, Per Orbem. 1925. 252p.

Heydte, Friedrich August von der.

Luftbombardement (In Wörterbuch des völkerrechts. Berlin, Gruyter, 1961, vol. 2, pp. 436-37)

Luftkriegsrecht (In Wörterbuch des völkerrechts. Berlin, Gruyter, 1961, vol. 2, pp. 438-41)

Luftkriegsregeln, Haager von 1923 (In Wörterbuch des völkerrechts. Berlin, Gruyter, 1961, vol. 2, pp. 441-42)

Heydte, Friedrich August von der and others. Le problème que pose l'existence des armes de destruction massive et la distinction entre les objectifs militaires et non militaires en général. 1967. 52 (II) Ann. de l'Institut de Droit International 1-271.

Johnson, D. H. N. Rights in air space. Manchester, Manchester Univ. Press; Dobbs Ferry, N.Y., Oceana. 1965. 129p.

Kroell, Joseph. Traité de droit international public aérien. Paris, Les Editions Internationales. 1936. Tome II, L'Aéronautique en temps de guerre, La · Guerre Aérienne. 533p.

Kruse, Hans. Bombardement (In Wörterbuch des völkerrechts. Berlin, Gruyter, 1961, vol. 1, pp. 222-23)

Le Goff, M. La guerre aérienne. 1955. 18 Rev. Générale de l'Air 165-90.

Leroy, Howard S. Limitation of air warfare. 1941. 12 Air L. Rev. 19-33.

Lin Wo-chiang. Aeronautical law in time of war. 1932. 3 J. Air L. 79-92.

Manisty, Herbert F. Aerial warfare and the laws of war. 1921. 7 Grotius Soc'y 33-41.

Mateesco, Nicolas. Traité de droit aérien-aéronautique; évolution, problèmes spatiaux. 2 éd. Paris, A. Pedone. 1964. (Deuxième partie, La réglementation juridique aérienne en fonction de la guerre, pp. 91-129)

Meyer, Alex. Völkerrechtlicher schutz der friedlichen personen und sachen gegen luftangriffe; das geltende kriegsrecht. Königsberg, Pr., und Berlin, Ost-Europa-Verlag. 1935. 257p.

Ming-Min Pen. Les bombardements aériens et la population civile depuis la seconde guerre mondiale: la bombe atomique. 1952. 15 (n.s.) Rev. Générale de l'air 302-11.

Missoffe, S. Le statut juridique de l'aéronef militaire (In Société internationale de droit pénal militaire et de droit de la guerre. 2. Congrès, Florence, 1961. L'aéronef militaire et le droit des gens: subordination et coopération militaire internationale, pp. 37-45, Strasbourg, 1963)

Phillips, C. P. Air warfare and the law; an analysis of the legal doctrines, practices and policies. 1953. 21 Geo. Wash. L. Rev. 311-35, 395-422.

La protection des populations civiles contre les bombardements; consultations juridiques de A. Hammerskjöld, Sir George Macdonogh, M. W. Royse, Vittorio Scialoja, Marcel Sibert, Walter Simons, jonkheer van Eysinga, A. Züblin. Genève, Au Siege du Comité International de la Croix-Rouge. 1930. 355p.

Quindry, Frank E. Aerial bombardment of civilian and military objectives. 1931. 2 J. Air L. 474-509.

Rodgers, William L. The laws of war concerning aviation and radio. 1923. 17 Am. J. Int'l L. 629-40.

Royse, Morton W. Aerial bombardment and the international regulation of warfare. New York, H. Vinal. 1928. 256p.

Sandiford, Roberto. Evolution du droit de la guerre maritime et aérienne (In Hague, Academy of international law. Recueil des cours 1939, 11, vol. 68, pp. 555-686)

Schwarzenberger, Georg. The law of air warfare and the trend towards total war. 1959. 1 U. Malaysia L. Rev. 120-36; 8 Am. U. L. Rev. 1-18.

Sibert, Marcel. Remarques et suggestions sur la protection des populations civiles contre les bombardements aériens. 1955. 59 Rev. Générale de Droit International Public 177-92.

Sloutzky, N. Le bombardement aérien des objectifs militaires. 1957. 61 Rev. Générale de Droit International Public 353-81.

Spaight, James M.
Air power and the cities. London, Longmans, Green. 1930. 244p.
Air power and war rights. 3d ed. New York, Longmans, Green. 1947. 523p.
Non-combatants and air attack. 1938. 9 Air L. Rev. 372-76.

Tapia Salinas, L. El derecho actual de la guerra aérea. 1961. 1 Jornadas de Derecho Penal Militar y Derecho de la Guerra 437-78.

Thomson, George R. Aerial attack and bombardment. 1936. 48 Jurid. Rev. 48-56.

Wilhelm, René Jean. Les conventions de Genève et la guerre aérienne. Genève. 1952. 33p.

Williams, Paul Whitcomb. Legitimate targets in aerial bombardment. 1929. 23 Am. J. Int'l L. 570-81.

Belligerent Occupation

Baxter, Richard R. The duty of obedience to the belligerent. 1950. 27 Brit. Yb. Int'l L. 235-66.

Colby, Elbridge. Occupation under the laws of war. 1925. 25 Colum. L. Rev. 904-22; 26: 146-70.

Debbasch, O. L'occupation militaire. Paris, Pichon et Durand-Auzias. 1961. 424p.

Feilchenfeld, Ernst H. The international economic law of belligerent occupation. Washington, Carnegie Endowment for International Peace. 1942. 181p.

Glahn, Gerhard von. The occupation of enemy territory . . . a commentary on the law and practice of belligerent occupation. Minneapolis, Univ. of

Minnesota Press. 1957. 350p.

Graber, Doris Appel. The development of the law of belligerent occupation 1863-1914. A historical survey. New York, Columbia Univ. Press. 1949. 343p.

Gutteridge, Joyce A. C. The rights and obligations of an occupying power. 1952. 6 Yb. World Aff. 149-69.

Hill, David J. The rights of the civil population in territory occupied by a belligerent. 1917. 11 Am. J. Int'l L. 133-37.

Hopkinson, Alfred (Sir). The treatment of civilians in occupied territories (In Grotius Society. Problems of war. . . . London, Sweet & Maxwell, 1917, vol. II, pp. 157-60)

Jamieson, Harvey. The law of belligerent occupation. 1945. 57 Jurid. Rev. 6-17.

Kido, Masahiko. The doctrine of military objective. 1961. 5 Japanese Ann. Int'l L. 39-44.

Lubrano-Lavadera, Eugène Michel. Les lois de la guerre et de l'occupation militaire. Préf. de Charles Rousseau. Paris, Charles-Lavauzelle. 1956. 143p.

Oppenheim, L. The legal relations between an occupying power and the inhabitants. 1917. 33 L.Q. Rev. 363-70.

Schwarzenberger, Georg. The law of belligerent occupation: basic issues. 1960. 30 Nordisk Tidsskrift for International Ret 10-24.

Wilson, Arnold (Sir). The laws of war in occupied territory. 1932. 18 Grotius Soc'y 17-39.

Wright, Rt. Hon Lord. The killing of hostages as a war crime. 1948. 25 Brit. Yb. Int'l L. 296-310.

Chemical-Biological Warfare

Bernstein, Cyrus. The law of chemical warfare. 1942. 10 Geo. Wash. L. Rev. 889-915.

Biological warfare—two views. United States use of biological warfare, W. H. Neinast; Status of biological warfare in international law, B. J. Brungs. April 1964. 1964. 24 Mil. L. Rev. 1-96.

Brooksbank, Alan. Chemical (gas) warfare and the law. 1937. 11 Austl. L.J. 125-31.

Bunn, George. Banning poison gas and germ warfare: should the United States agree? 1969. Wis. L. Rev. 375-420.

Conference for the Supervision of the International Trade in Arms and Ammunition and in Implements of War, Geneva, 1925. Protocol for the prohibition of the use in war of asphyxiating, poisonous or other gases and of bacteriological methods of warfare. Signed at Geneva, June 17, 1925. Canadian ratification deposited May 6, 1930. Ottawa, F. A. Acland, Printer to the King. 1931. 8p.

Conference on Chemical and Biological Warfare, London, 1968. CBW: chemical and biological warfare. Edited by Steven Rose with the assistance of David Pavett. Boston, Beacon Press. 1969. 209p.

Ewing, Russel H. The legality of chemical warfare. 1927. 61 Am. L. Rev. 58-76.

Herriott, R. M. Biological warfare (In Barker, C. A. Problems of world dis-

110

armament. Boston, Houghton, Mifflin, 1963, pp. 68-81)

Hinz, Joachim. Bakteriologische kriegführung (In Wörterbuch des völkerrechts. Berlin, Gruyter, 1961, vol. 1, pp. 140-41)

Kelly, J. B. Gas warfare in international law. 1960. 9 Mil. L. Rev. 1.

Krickus, R. J. On the morality of chemical biological warfare. 1965. 9 J. Conflict Resolution 200-10.

Kruse, Hans. Gaskrieg (In Wörterbuch des völkerrechts. Berlin, Gruyter, 1961, vol. 1, pp. 615-16)

Lasagna, Louis. Chemical warfare (In Barker, C. A. Problems of world disarmament. Boston, Houghton, Mifflin, 1963, pp. 61-68)

Lieberman, E. J. Psychochemicals as weapons. 1962. 18 (1) Bull. Atomic Scientists 11-14.

McCarthy, Richard D. The ultimate folly: war by pestilence, asphyxiation and defoliation. New York, Knopf. 1969. 176p

Meyrowitz, Henri.
Les armes biologiques et le droit international. Paris, Pedone. 1968. 157p.
Les armes psychochimiques et le droit international. 1964. 10 Annuaire Français de Droit International 81-126.

O'Brien, William V. Biological/chemical warfare and the international law of war. 1962. 51 Geo. L. J. 1-63.

Pfalzgraff, R. L., jr. Biological and chemical weapons. 1964. 47 Current Hist. 18-24.

Sack, Alexander N. ABC—atomic, biological, chemical warfare in international law. 1950. 10 Law. Guild Rev. 161-80.

Schelling, T. C. War without pain and other models. 1963. 15 World Pol. 465-87.

Thomas, Ann (Van Wynen) and Thomas, A. J., jr. Development of international legal limitations on the use of chemical and biological weapons. Dallas, Southern Methodist Univ. School of Law. 1968. 2v.

United Nations. Department of Political and Security Council Affairs. Chemical and bacteriological (biological) weapons and the effects of their possible use; report of the Secretary-general. New York. 1969. 100p. (A/7575/Rev. 1; S/9292/Rev. 1)

U.S. Congress. House. Comm. on Foreign Affairs (91.1). Chemical-biological warfare: U.S. policies and international effects. Hearings before subcommittee on national security policy and scientific developments, Nov. 18, 20; Dec. 2, 9, 18 & 19, 1969. Washington, Gov't Print. Off. 1970. 513p.

U.S. Congress. House. Comm. on Government Operations (91.1). Environmental dangers of open-air testing of lethal chemicals. Tenth report . . . Washington, Gov't Print. Off. 1969. 62p.

Limited and Unconventional Warfare

Baldwin, G. B. New look at the law of war: limited war and field manual 27-10. April 1959. Mil. L. Rev. 1.

De Beco, Véronique. Application des conventions de Genève dans les guerres non conventionnelles. 1966. 52 Int'l L. Ass'n Conf. Rep. 703-08.

Greenberg, E. V. C. Law and the conduct of the Algerian revolution. 1970.

11 Harv. Int'l L. J. 37-72.
Greenspan, Morris. International law and its protection for participants in unconventional warfare. May 1962. 341 Annals 30-41.
International committee and the Viet Nam conflict. 1966. 6 Int'l Rev. Red Cross 399-418.
Kelly, Joseph B. Legal aspects of military operations in counterinsurgency. July 1963. 21 Mil. L. Rev. 95-122.
Kelly, Joseph B. and Pelletier, George A., jr. Legal control of populations in subversive warfare. 1965. 5 Va. J. Int'l L. 174-200.
Meyrowitz, Henri. Le droit de la guerre dans le conflit vietnamien. 1967. 13 Annuaire Français de Droit International 153-201.
Nurick, Lester and Barrett, Roger W. Legality of guerilla forces under the laws of war. 1946. 40 Am J. Int'l L. 563-83.
Santos, Guillermo S. The rule of law in unconventional warfare. 1965. 40 Philippine L. J. 455-74.
Shull, Lewis F. Counterinsurgency and the Geneva conventions—some practical considerations. 1968. 3 Int'l Law. 49-57.
Siotis, Jean. Le droit de la guerre et les conflits armés d'un caractère non-international. Paris, Librairie Générale de Droit et de Jurisprudence. 1958. 248p.
Trainin, I. P. Questions of guerilla warfare in the law of war. 1946. 40 Am. J. Int'l L. 534-62.

Nuclear Weapons

Abdel-Hamid, S. Quelques réflexions sur la legalité des activités atomiques. 1966. Annuario di Diritto Internazionale 105-31.
Bright, Fred, jr. Nuclear weapons as a lawful means. 1965. 30 Mil. L. Rev. 1-42.
Brownlie, Ian. Some legal aspects of the use of nuclear weapons. 1965. 14 Int'l & Comp. L. Q. 437-51.
Charlier, R. E. Questions juridiques soulevées par l'évolution de la science atomique (In Hague. Academy of international law 1957, I, vol. 91, pp. 213-381)
Euler, Alexander. Die atomwaffe im luftkriegsrecht. Köln, Carl Heymanns Verlag. 1960. 200p.
Falk, Richard A.
The Shimoda case: a legal appraisal of the atomic attacks upon Hiroshima and Nagasaki. 1965. 59 Am. J. Int'l L. 759-93.
The Shimoda case: a legal appraisal of the atomic attacks upon Hiroshima and Nagasaki (In Gross, Leo, ed. International law in the twentieth century. N.Y., Appleton-Century-Crofts, 1969, pp. 733-67)
Gotlieb, A. E. Nuclear weapons in outer space. 1965. 3 Can. Yb. Int'l L. 3-35.
Heydte, Friedrich A. F. von der.
Atomare kriegführung und völkerrecht. 1961. 9 Archiv des Völkerrechts 162-82.
Exposé sur l'état des travaux de la cinquième commission: le problème que pose l'existence des armes de destruction massive et la distinction entre objectifs militaires et non militaires. 1967. 52 (2) Annuaire de l'Institut

de Droit International 527-33.

Mallison, W. T., jr. The laws of war and the judicial control of weapons of mass destruction in general and limited wars. 1967. 36 Geo. Wash. L. Rev. 308-46.

Menon, P. K. Nuclear weapons and modern rules of war. 1966. 2 (5-6) Civ. & Mil. L. J. 22-46.

Menzel, Eberhard. Legalität oder illegalität der anwendung von atomwaffen. Tübingen, J. C. B. Mohr. 1960. 87p.

Meyrowitz, Henri. Les juristes devant l'arme nucléaire. 1963. 67 Rev.Générale de Droit International Public 820-73.

O'Brien, W. W.
Legitimate military necessity in nuclear war. 1960. 2 World Polity 35-120.
Some problems of the law of war in limited nuclear warfare. Oct. 1961. Mil. L. Rev. 1.

Pessoa, Mário. Leis da guerra e armas nucleares. São Paulo, Editôra Revista dos Tribunais. 1969. 362p.

Radojkovic, Milŏs. Les armes nucléaires et le droit international. 1962. Yb. World Aff. 197-215.

Rubio Garcia, L.
Guerra atómica, guerra limitada y politica desatomizacion un aspecto de la crisis de la humanización bélica. 1960. 13 Revista Española de Derecho Internacional 418-515.
La guerra nuclear: moral, derecho y política en la época atómica. 1965. 20 Revista Espanola de Derecho Militar 9-34.

Schwarzenberger, Georg. The legality of nuclear weapons. London, Stevens. 1958. 70p.

Setalvad, M. C. Nuclear weapons and international law. 1963. 3 Indian J. Int'l L. 383-95.

Singh, N. Nuclear weapons and international law. London, Stevens. 1959. 267p.

Sloutzky, N. La population civile devant la menace de destruction massive. 1955. 59 Rev. Générale de Droit International Public 218-45.

Smith, H. A. Modern weapons and modern war. 1955. 9 Yb. World Aff. 222-47.

Stowell, Ellery C. The laws of war and the atomic bomb. 1945. 39 Am. J. Int'l L. 784-88.

Prisoners of War

Kunz, Josef L. Treatment of prisoners of war. 1953. 47 Am. Soc'y Int'l L. Proc. 99-121.

Levie, Howard S.
Maltreatment of prisoners of war in Vietnam. 1968. 48 B. U. L. Rev. 323-59.
Penal sanctions for maltreatment of prisoners of war. 1962. 56 Am. J. Int'l L. 433-68.
Prisoners of war and the protecting power. 1961. 55 Am. J. Int'l L. 374-97.

McGinness, John R. An international bill of rights for prisoners of war. 1953.

2 Clev.-Mar. L. Rev. 158-65.

Maresca, A. La condizione giuridica dei prigionieri di guerra. 1961. 28 Revista di Studi Politici Internazionali 97-112.

Standard minimum rules for the treatment of prisoners. 1969. 2 N.Y.U. J. Int'l L. & Pol. 314-32.

Protection of Civilians

Castrén, Erik J. S.

Necessité et possibilite' de la protection juridique de la population civile dans la guerre moderne (In Estudios de derecho internacional homenaje a D. Antonio de Luna. Madrid, 1968, pp. 496-507)

Necessite' et possibilite' de la protection juridique de la population civile dans la guerre moderne. 1968. 21 Revista Española de Derecho Internacional 647-58.

La protection juridique de la population civile dans la guerre moderne. 1955. 59 Rev. Générale de Droit International Public 121-36.

Coursier, Henri. Etudes sur la formation du droit humanitaire. Genève, Journal du Genève. 1952. 106p.

Droit de la guerre et droit humanitaire: pour la relance des idées de la protection de la population civile en temps de guerre. 1963. 9 Annales de Droit International Médical 48-61.

Hammer, Ellen and Salvin, Marina. The taking of hostages in theory and practice. 1944. 38 Am. J. Int'l L. 20-33.

Helm, Johann Georg. Die rechtsstellung der zivilbevölkerung im kriege in ihrer geschichtlichen entwicklung ein beitung zur geschichte des völkerrechts. Frankfurt am Main. 1957. 135p.

Lot of the civilian population in war-time. 1966. 6 Int'l Rev. Red Cross 79-89.

Maresca, A. La protezione internazionale dei combattenti e dei civili. Milano, Giuffrè. 1965. 290p.

Mudge, George Alfred. Starvation as a means of warfare. 1970. 4 Int'l Law. 228-68.

Nurick, Lester.

The distinction between combatant and noncombatant in the law of war. 1945. 39 Am. J. Int'l L. 680-97.

The distinction between combatant and noncombatant in the law of war (In Gross, Leo, ed. International law in the twentieth century. N.Y., Appleton-Century-Crofts, 1969, pp. 667-84)

Papelier, Philippe. Le droit de la guerre et la population civile. Thèse, Paris. 213p.

La protection des populations civiles contre les bombardements; consultations juridiques de A. Hammersköld, Sir George Macdonogh, M. W. Royse, Vittorio Scialoja, Marcel Sibert, Walter Simons, jonkheer van Eysinga, A. Zublin. Genève, Au Siège du Comité International de la Croix-Rouge. 1930. 253p.

Protection of civilian population in times of conflict. 1965. 5 Int'l Rev. Red Cross 655-61.

Protection of civilian populations against the dangers of indiscriminate war-

fare. 1967. 7 Int'l Rev. Red Cross 300-11.
Red Cross. International Committee, Geneva.
  Draft rules for the limitation of the dangers incurred by the civilian
    population in time of war. 2d ed. Geneva. 1958. 170p.
  Draft rules for the protection of the civilian population from the dangers
    of indiscriminate warfare; introduction, text and commentary. Geneva.
    1955.
  Projet de règles limitant les risques courus par la population civile en temps
    de guerre. Genève. 1956. 166p. 115p.
  Final record concerning the draft rules for the limitation of the dangers
    incurred by the civilian population in time of war. Geneva. 1958. 184p.
Seidl-Hohenveldern, I. et Patrnogic, J. La protection des populations civiles
  dans les conflits armés de caractère non international. 1968. 17 Annales de
  Droit International Médical 12-24.

Relief of the Sick and Wounded

Andereff, Margrit. Die schutzbestimmungen in den internationalen
  abkommen über das Rote Kreuz. St. Gallen, Zollikofer. 1941. 122p.
Clémens, René. Le projet de Monaco; le droit et la guerre, villes sanitaires et
  villes de securité, assistance sanitaire internationale. Bruxelles, E. Bruylant.
  1937. 307p.
Jakovljevic, B. The protection of the wounded and sick and the development
  of international medical law. 1965. 5 Int'l Rev. Red Cross 115-22.
Patrnogic, Jovica. Application des règles du droit international médical con-
  tenus dans les conventions de Genève concernant les conflits internes.
  1966. 52 Int'l L. Ass'n Conf. 684-89.
Lapradelle, P. de.
  The protection of medical aircraft in time of conflict. 1967. 7 Int'l Rev.
    Red Cross 459-72.
  Le statut de l'aviation sanitaire. 1966. 29 Rev. Générale d'Air 261-71.

115